Love Songs from the Boogeymen

HARPER'S
MAGAZINE
PRESS

Love Songs from the

Boogeymen

by Judith Trotsky

HARPER'S MAGAZINE PRESS
Published in Association with Harper & Row
New York

Grateful acknowledgment is hereby made to the following for permission to reprint the material specified:

Excerpts on page 90 from Max Lerner's column which appeared in the June 1, 1966 issue of the New York *Post*, reprinted by permission of the author.

Excerpts from *The Love Song of J. Alfred Prufrock* by T.S. Eliot are reprinted from his volume *Collected Poems 1909–1962* by permission of Harcourt Brace Jovanovich, Inc; copyright © 1936, by Harcourt Brace Jovanovich, Inc; copyright © 1963, 1964, by T.S. Eliot, and Faber and Faber Ltd.

Lyrics from *The Sweetheart of Sigma Chi.* Lyric by Byron D. Stokes. Music by F. Dudleigh Vernor. Copyright 1912 by Richard E. Vernor Publishing Co. Copyright renewed and assigned to Edwin H. Morris & Company, Inc. Used by permission.

Excerpts from article entitled "Out of the South—A Hero-at-Large" by John Neary originally appeared in *LIFE* Magazine. © 1968 Time Inc.

Excerpts from "Private Worlds," "Night Falls on the City," and "A Place in the Country" by Sarah Gainham reprinted by permission of Holt, Rinehart and Winston, Inc.

"Harper's" is the registered trademark of Harper & Row, Publishers, Inc.

FIRST EDITION

Designed by Gloria Adelson

Library of Congress Cataloging in Publication Data

Trotsky, Judith.
  Love songs from the boogeymen.
  1. Trotsky, Judith. I. Title.
PN1992.4.T7A3   818'.5'403 [B]   73–6313
ISBN 0–06–128200–6

*To Betty Lauterstein Trotsky and Maurice Trotsky,
for and by whom Liberty was built*

Contents

NOTE ix

BOOK ONE:

I HEAR AMERICA SINGING 1

BOOK TWO:

GENERATIONS OF SILENCE 61

BOOK THREE:

THE CASUALTIES OF WAR 119

AN EPILOGUE 165

Acknowledgments

These are the people who made the pictures which appear on all the pages following:

Eleanor Fogelson and John Atkinson, David Chertok and Bernard Chertok, Irving Greenberg, Leah A. Kramer. And, of course, William J. Fienemann, John Tebbel and Walter Marek, great teachers and great gentlemen who, each in his own way, drew all the outlines for this work.

Note

This is the last week of March, early spring of 1973. We are 27.6 years away from rediscovery of The Slab: the quantum leap of knowledge projected for *2001*. Or are we already there?

Man is the only organism capable of contemplating itself; and our own reflections change us all. Multiple minds now combine to conceive new forms. They devise a language whose piercing concentrates of sound affect the structure of the very brains that invent the words. Out of the dimness of the past, in the present, man creates something man has never heard before.

Evolution has a primal principle: Ontogeny recapitulates philogeny. In the growth from fetal form to final birth, the individual traces the evolution that has led to him.

But we must now formulate a further phrase. For in the world that we have made, the intercourse of intellects evolves the intellects involved.

We do not yet hear the prophecy. But the images are very clear. The movies, too, were silent first.

Book One

I Hear America Singing

🪝 1

Interstate 95 is one of the inexorable probes that reach, like filaments of a concrete web, across the face of America today. At the
southern end of Interstate 95 is Florida's east coast. Interstate 95
is, in fact, a coastal road, an updated version of U.S. 1, which we
have long since outgrown. The massive turnpike then roughly
follows the irregular line of the Atlantic coast, passing the in-
dented erosion of the Potomac River, at whose northern end
the District of Columbia sits. From Washington, Interstate 95
threads irregularly through the state of New Jersey, leaning
sometimes still on U.S. 1. It crosses the city of New York in the
Bronx, then begins its long journey up through the New England
states, departing the sea, finally, just north of Portland to continue to Canada through east central Maine.

On July 19, 1969, Leah and I are on Interstate 95. Enclosed in
my automobile, we are tacking to the state of Maine, enduring,
through endless motion, the last summer of this most terrible
decade. We have a rendezvous to keep. Children of our land,
nothing must keep us from the event. Nothing can.

It is a hot Saturday afternoon. Caught in the sclerotic traffic,
my car breaks down on the Portsmouth Bridge. Though she is as

unnerved as I am, Leah only says—as she has often said these last ten years—"Everything I touch turns to shit."

We are, however, women who have been, who have had to be, crisis trained; and, though it involves a delay of many hours and a circuitous, anxious drive through side roads to Kennebunkport, we are able to find someone, finally, to fix the car. The only mechanic willing to respond lives and works in a ramshackle series of barns set in a garden long since overgrown. We enter through a dusty road, past a shallow arch of trees. It is like no garage I have ever seen. Children scatter laughing through the yard, cars are parked untidily about: images of a distant cousin's rural chicken farm blip upon my memory.

The setting is most unmechanical; but the man who owns it is quick, precise and skilled in diagnosing the ills of this automobile I have already come to hate. It had broken down before, and patient Leah was with me then as well. That had been at the beginning of June, the first day of my ownership.

The mechanic works like the legendary detective in stories I had read and heard long ago. Reasoning inductively, quickly he eliminates possibilities that are not the cause. Stooping over the shimmering engine, he dips his fingers into the little pool which has collected in the curving metal well of the frame. He smells and tastes and reasons what it is.

"Radiator cap don't fit," he says. "See if I can find you one." And off he goes to rummage laconically through bits and pieces of metal scattered all about the place. Replacing my new cap with an older one, he fits it and off we go much relieved. The bill has been four dollars. Under the warranty I will collect it from the company. But it is only the first of many, and many which I will not collect. The car, the mechanism to quiet my restlessness, the gift I have awarded myself for a decade of difficult work; the car, the American mobile, breaks down again and again for the next several years. It only happens when I am going away.

But then, for the next several years, I am always going away.

In early evening, the evening before our rendezvous, we decide to leave Interstate 95. It has been designed to carry us most efficiently to Bangor, the last turnpike landmark before a southeast reach to Bar Harbor, Maine, where we have made reservations for a television set. But we are tired of technological marvels, landscaped by planted trees, hiding from us the countryside we have never seen and of which we are so much a part. And so we swing to the old-fashioned alternative, U.S. 1, which hugs Maine's coast from Bath to Newcastle; from Belfast to beyond. The names are our heritage, and the road, like time, twists and curves. Bath, Newcastle, Belfast. Memorials to a past which still exists. Like the space explorer in his symbolized, windowless room, we have only to fix our gaze to see what we will be and what we have also been. In the windshield mirror the road curves back. The corrected engine hums, carrying us within our room. On the horizon there is another world.

In Marks, Mississippi, they have harnessed the mules in a sea of mud: spring rain falls on the verdant South. The Flood has begun, but on this day in 1968 there is only a trickle issuing from the dam. We cannot yet believe our walls will fall.

In the muddy, unplowed field an old woman in a vast, flapping orange coat with dolman sleeves is heaved into the wagon by an elderly, bone-taut man. He watches her struggles as she tries to fit herself onto the narrow, rough-hewn boards. On his face the newsreel camera records a male incredulity that is as old as man himself.

They are ready to begin. The night before, someone has stolen the mules: thirty-two were taken, thirty-one returned. To the camera the young man says: "We are not going to riot. We are a nonviolent organization. We are going to continue to be a nonviolent organization. But we are not going to sell our manhood."

Manhood is found as it was a century before, and if there is anachronism here, the wagon train is more poignant now, moving down the wet concrete streets of Marks, trailed by honking automobiles. The rain continues. In the script it is a foreshadowing of things to come.

On the neat and open porch of a small house sheltered by Mississippi trees, two women watch as the wagons pass. They

5

have chosen to stay at home and stand underneath the dripping roof, waiting, perhaps, for the rain to stop. Still, they must have had some destination in mind. One of them wears a bright pink hat.

Thirteen wagons pass, beginning a journey that will take twenty-six days, the reporter says. (The network has sent a black to this seminal Mississippi point.) As they pass, as lines of them are picked up by cameras on turnpikes and small-town roads, as they plod slowly among the impatient cars and traffic jams, they bear these signs hand-lettered on their white-sheet coverings:

"You Can't Kill All of Us. Stop the War"

"I Have Seen The Promise Land"

"I Have a dream"

"What Is Better? Send Man To Moon or Feed Him on Earth?"

Later the reporter is to interview one of the pioneers, an old man who wears his brown felt hat pushed back upon his head. What did the neighbors say, the reporter asks, about the old man's march on Washington?

The old man is Mississippi-born.

"Said they get you up there they beat you to death."

Threading our way through the last New England towns, we spot a white frame restaurant sitting on a pier and enter it to watch the sun go down while we have an evening meal. A single sail floats, postcard style, on the shadowing estuary. We are both silent, and if Leah is filled with thoughts which say "I wish . . ." she keeps her sadnesses to herself. As I keep mine.

The water is surrounded by a thicket of pines which reach down to its banks; richly foliaged, the trees circle the irregular shore. Dark green, almost black, the evening waters meld, land and water line becoming indistinct. Above, striations of clouds turn neon, coralized by the setting sun. Dimly seen, the outlines of the moon begin to sharpen, heightened by the blackening sky.

I am not thinking much. Watching, with an American land-scape filling the entire retina of my eye, I hear snatches of music I have not sung since I was a child. We stood in assembly then, faces turned to the flag as the honor guard marched down the aisle; and raised our young voices earnestly in an opening hymn of praise:

> O beautiful for spacious skies,
> For amber waves of grain,
> For purple mountain majesties
> Above the fruited plain!

To us, at the time, it was little more than ritual; and the flag which bobbed down the aisle, carried by the tallest, strongest boy, was merely the tricolor of our national team.

> America! America!
> God shed his grace on thee
> And crown thy good with brotherhood
> From sea to shining sea!

But if they were, then, only part of an obligatory rite, there was also no shame in singing them. I would not sing them now. But I cannot help hearing as the song plays on.

"I hear America singing," Walt Whitman said, writing of another time. But now the only sound left to hear is a dulled, humming noise behind the hushed concatenations of the room.

It is a summer weekend; and clean, tanned bodies, casually dressed, speak softly as the laden plates are delivered, as drinks are served, the ice tinkling musically. On the tables, the colored, wax-filled bowls are set aglow by waitresses flourishing long wooden matches which they dip into the glass to catch an already used, blackened wick. Soft candlelight bathes the room as the sun goes down; and a gracious land continues its civilities among the little pools of light.

"I hear America singing," Walt Whitman wrote, 109 years before.

"Singing, with open mouths, their strong melodious songs."

Several lifetimes have passed since. We are different than we were.

Leah and I gaze out into the dark; hands clasped in front of us. We do not gesture, we do not squirm. We do not speak. What is there to say? We wait, quietly, patiently, though our meal takes a long time to prepare. We have been gentle-raised; and with gentility we endure. It has been a long and tiring day, strapped into our seats, constantly on the move. But we fit well within the scene: our travel clothes are wrinkle-proof. We are two young women journeying . . . alone. In the hush of the room where we sit, unmoving, grateful to be still, the music sings: words I have forgotten that I once knew.

> O beautiful for pilgrim feet,
> Whose stern, impassioned stress
> A thoroughfare for freedom beat
> Across the wilderness

Finally the meal arrives. We are overhungry, but it is well worth the wait. Silently, absorbed, we eat: a dozen steamed clams apiece; New England chowder, rich, butter-laden, thick with meats; Caesar salad from a monumental bowl; broiled lobsters which we crack open daintily, picking all the cavities bare; baked potato, with sour cream and chives which we spoon on luxuriously; an assortment of vegetables.

Steadily, concentrating, we continue our passage to dessert, which the smiling waitress proudly brings, bearing the tray before her, holding the precious crown of our feast. It is a basket-load of fresh strawberries, piled on squares of cake, covered with a billowing swirl of real whipped cream. A single perfect piece of fruit nestles on the top: a jewel: an insignia.

We cannot eat another bite. Yet, we do. And have our coffee afterward; as other plates are pushed away; as the bowl candles flicker; as darkness descends outside, hiding a silent world.

> America! America!
> God mend thine every flaw,
> Confirm thy soul in self-control,
> Thy liberty in law

"I hear America singing," the poet said. But the song, like our bodies puffed with food, functions only fitfully; as if the rotary mechanism on a phonograph had, somehow, off-centered itself and the melody lurches for a moment in speed and then slows;

and the single word "America!" trills triumphantly, a grace-noted theme, while what follows becomes distorted into a moan; an inhuman sound of primitive speech: a long, anguished cry of pain.

Rising finally, pulling our sluggish bodies up, we continue with our drive. We have, still, a long way to go. Readjusting the seat belts as we set out for the Bar Harbor Motor Inn, Leah says, "Do you want me to talk to you?" It is late. We have overeaten. She is afraid I will fall asleep.

It is unnecessary. I seldom speak. I have been silent for many years. Motion is my language now. And, throbbing steadily to the east, undistracted by an intrusive present, I can enjoy my own picture show and let loose all the fragmented scenes; create my own dialogue and play all the parts as I direct myself; cutting the score as I will, discarding music's rules.

I live within my own created land. Lifting each word, each image, each private sound from its recording reel, I can, with my will alone, contemplate before assigning each to its peg above the bin: discard, keep, keep, maybe. Sometimes I think a long time before I decide, wondering where this scene will lead. I offer myself a kaleidoscope of choice. Which picture do I wish to see today? Where do I wish to go?

> Thine alabaster cities gleam,
> Undimmed by human tears.

I don't much care. The music is distorted. Long ago I lost the beat.

"I hear America singing," the poet said. Deafened in America, now I hear . . . nothing at all.

The monuments of Washington appear flat and painted on behind the ragged circle that has congregated in impromptu audience. The man, middle-aged, is wearing a red cardigan sweater and a white shirt, with a large button pinned beneath his heart. On the button is a picture of Martin Luther King, in death campaigning still. The murder was only a month before.

The man points skyward. "They say believe in God."

"Yeah!" the audience answers back.

9

"I believe in God," he says.

"Yeah," the response comes again.

"But where is God? Where is Jesus?" Legs astride, hands on hips, he proclaims:

"I am black."

"Yeah!"

"I am proud to be black!"

"Yeah!"

"My Momma bore me black!"

"Yeah!"

"And all of us here is black!"

"Yeah!"

"And so"—he pauses—"why should we be ashamed?"

". . . No." The group breaks stride. Pieces of response are scattered through the audience. Motionless, seated on the grass, they mutely watch as the preacher continues haranguing them.

In another part of the City, a young woman talks to television's representatives. "We are here because we're trod down a lot," she says. "We're poor in spirit as well as wealth." Young and pretty, she wears a sweat shirt carrying the insignia of NYU.

There is a more formal scene, played in front of microphones and cameras for all the world to see. The Reverend Ralph David Abernathy speaks a prayer:

"We are come from the north, we are come from the south. We are come from the east and we are come from the west."

A jet cracks overhead. He must pause. Then:

"We are going to plague the pharaohs of this nation with plague after plague. . . ."

Concluding his speech, Abernathy drives first nails into A-framed shacks: visualized symbol like the Golden Spike, of which we now have only stored daguerreotypes to remind us of that moment in time when we were, geographically, joined.

On another part of the field, the newsmen do color interviews.

"Been livin' hard all my life," the old man says.

The living is no easier here: testimony, protest, marches.

Rain. The planked sidewalks sink into fields of mud. The barefoot residents tune dials in transistor radios: clapping hands,

10

they do a mired boogaloo. Children huddle under the plywood tents, trying to keep dry. Knee-deep, Resurrection City carries on. Dignitaries come to see for themselves; and close in filmed discussions with the instruments of testament.

On June 24, 1968, the permit expires. Resurrection City is, forcibly, hauled away.

Abernathy speaks:

"Resurrection City was not a mistake, and the rain was not a mistake and the mud which came about as a result of the rain was not a mistake... There is a force in this country that is alive more than many of us realize, and ... we are going to save this nation. We are going to save it in spite of itself."

Protesting, illegalized by lack of permit, Abernathy spends twenty days in jail. He fasts "in a gesture of identification with the poor and hungry."

The camera films his release through the fence of the prison yard. Black hands, clutching at the wire, are focused up. On the track, someone we cannot see says, "Look at him. He just like ... a lord!"

To the small crowd of supporters, remaining behind in Washington, the preacher talks again about "the dream of our founding fathers. ... There is still hunger in the land," he says. "But we have made the invisible visible. And never again will the poor be invisible in this country."

Abernathy's prophecy is made on July 13, 1968.

At the southern end of Interstate 95 is an impermanent city of another kind. Living there in tents, trailers, monumental camper trucks, one year later the citizens wait. They spread metal card tables in front of their temporary doors and stack them with coolers of beer and plates of fruit and sandwiches.

Groups have organized caravans. One station wagon bears the flag-and-star-encrusted sign: "Official Observers, Baltimore Gun Club. Happy Landings."

John Kennedy had asked: "Why go to the moon?"

A young, bare-chested Englishman says: "You can't spend all your money on the poor. You should spend a bit more. But you

11

can't stop going to the moon just because you've got poor."

There are other signs. "Closing the Space Between Man and God": the hubris of a church marquee; and, on the billboard of the Sheraton Cocoa Beach Resort Motor Inn, "The Whole World is Watching You Apollo."

The whole world is watching us.

At this moment in Budapest, a crowd gathers in front of an appliance store which has put one small television set in the window space. An old woman, babushkaed, wearing ragged gray ankle socks on her sandaled feet, watches intently, the cigarette forgotten between her callused fingertips.

Excitement ripples through the floating crowd on the Via Veneto. A waiter arcs his tray with balletomanic flourishes. "My wife, she's American," he says, serving with a luted élan. The restaurant has devised a celebrant dish they've christened "Moon Rocks." The wine-flavored specialty is cubed chunks of our native American fruit. On this day they serve watermelon in Rome.

In Piccadilly Circus the electric sign flashes its news between reminders for razor blades: "US LUNAR MODULE EAGLE SEPARATES FROM MOTHER SHIP." Spectators watch, human islands of motionlessness among the ribboned traffic's lights.

In the outdoor Japanese garden, all the metal tables are filled. Huge crisp Sony screens are set in open air. A Japanese in a silver space suit circulates among the crowd. In the park, a girl reporter, trailing a microphone cord, chases a young man harnessed to two giant balloons who is bobbing up and down in a dippy weightless walk.

At this moment, at the northern end of U.S. 95, we have gathered around the lobby set of the Bar Harbor Motor Inn. A crowd streams in from the street, grows behind, spreads in a semicircle ringing the corner of the room.

Eagle has separated. It reports: "We're going right down U.S. 1."

"It's grown quite quiet here in Mission Control."

The quiet layers continents.

"You are go for landing. Over," Houston says.

Hushed, tense, we hold our breaths. In Rome, in the red-plushed common room of the pensione, our scene duplicates itself.

"Roger, go for landing, three thousand feet. We're go. We're go. Two thousand feet. Two thousand feet. . . ."

In Bucharest they move inside the store and watch among the washing machines.

"Eagle, looking great. You're go."

The game has stopped in White Sox park. Heads bow in silent ritual. The world sends up a Babeled prayer.

"Altitude 1,600 . . . 1,400 feet, still looking very good."

I can barely see the screen. A well of tears clouds my eyes.

"Thirty-five degrees. Thirty-five degrees 750 coming down to twenty-three; two hundred feet twenty-one down. . . ."

In Rome, sensitive microphones pick up the ticking of a watch: the camera focuses on Mickey Mouse.

"Sixty seconds."

"Lights on; down two and a half. Forward, forward forty feet down two and a half picking up some dust; thirty feet two and a half down shadow, four forward, four forward, drifting to the right a little."

An old woman sits opposite me, face gray and drained. Her fingers clutch their knobby joints. She is as old as manned flight itself.

"Thirty seconds."

We do not breathe.

"Contact light. Okay engines stop. Engine arm off."

"We copy. You're down, Eagle."

Down. . . . On the moon!

"Tranquility Base here. The Eagle has landed."

A triumphant chorale issues from a billion throats. On the . . . moon! I am sobbing. I am not alone: flooded with feeling we cannot control. Courage: an American word. It has been a long time since I have heard this from an audience. But this time the brave heroes have not died their necessary deaths for us. Eagle, our Eagle is on the moon!

Getting up, I run outside, to flop down beside the pool. We have kept our rendezvous. And Tranquility Base sings to the world.

It has been a long and anxious journey to our large and comfortable motel room and we are very tired as we sit, propped by pyramids of pillows, in our beds viewing the television screen above our toes.

"You guys are getting prime time on TV there," Houston says.

It is prime time everywhere on earth. In a Japanese living room, a family is transfixed. Before them, on a low table, piles of reference works diagram the flight with charts and graphs.

Images waver before our eyes. "The hatch is coming open. Okay, Houston, I'm on the porch."

Leah's head nods toward the lamp on the night table between the beds.

"Up, up!" I command. She comes awake.

But, saturated by time, I find I am drowsing too.

"Halt where you are a minute, Neil," says the voice on the moon.

We have traveled far to reach this point, pushing at our obstacles. The mechanism of the will slows down, worn out. It must rest.

". . . foot of the ladder . . . powder . . . very fine."

Static voices recede. I drift off into space of my own. Leah is on the watch, but there is no conviction in her voice. The figure moves across the room in subliminal bursts of consciousness.

"One small step for man . . ."

Struggle to stay awake.

"One giant leap for mankind. . . ."

The battle is lost. It is the ending of an awesome decade. I am too weary to watch it anymore.

At this moment in Paris, a man is saying *"C'est fantastique. . . . It is something so deep I can't express."* In Paris, the reporter says, the French have stayed up throughout the night.

The television set stays on. But, unconscious, I am in a sound-proofed sleep.

The next morning Leah and I look at each other, slightly shamed. But I am able to rationalize my loss. Returning to work,

14

I will be able to see it all on film.

A few days later on a Canadian coast, an innkeeper welcomes us.

"You are Americans?" he says.

We nod apprehensively, wondering why he asks.

"We want to congratulate you. It is a wonderful thing that you have done."

And as we sign the register—our names, addresses, U.S.A.—I think that this is the first foreign journey in many years in which my citizenship has invoked some praise.

Tranquility Base is the construction of man. But it is our flag that is planted there, our colors visible from the moon.

O beautiful for heroes proved . . .

And on all the intrastates that we have, first filaments of pride appear again. They are fragile threads even yet. But the staff of anthems forms itself once again to build what we can hear:

Who more than self their country loved . . .

There is, perhaps, a resurrection from the ruins: familiar words and music are the foundations upon which we might construct.

And mercy more than life!

A new road: it will last a thousand years.

♫ 2

"Why go to the moon?" John Kennedy asked at the beginning of the decade; and, with a predictive aphorism, launched a nation into the minatory darknesses of interrelated space.

"Why go to the moon?" The answer to that was manifest. "Cross the sea? The world is flat!" We were, ourselves, the result of an unequivocal belief. And, in successive years, as I heard the question repeat and amplify, the historic progression was very clear: the risk of infinity in state-bought ships. Nearly five hundred years before, but was it not the same today? And I could, now that we were reaching too, comprehend more easily the kind of courage Columbus had in testing the limits of the world. He might have fallen off the edge. The discovery of Oz was the conquest of fear. All great explorations are.

"Why go to the moon?" One Friday night near the end of the decade, I took another sort of journey: into time . . . back to where time itself began.

It was late at night and, drowsing in the rear of the car, I was conscious of little movement except for the sway of the automobile as it carried us upward through the winding winter roads of

Vermont. We were alone, and our headlights lit the gnarled trees which looked like the wreckage of some other world upon which a dread sentence had been carried out.

Wrapped in a billowing ski parka, like a down comforter, I was gently rocked, cradled in an amniotic fluid of transition forms: not yet born. Once, somewhere during those hours, sleepily I cleared a space with a leather-mittened hand and looked out on the desolated scene. It was one million years B.C.

We had come to the edge of a giant icecap that moved imperceptibly from the ends of the earth, extruding between the valleys of wild and dangerous mountain peaks. There were no generations past and I was, at that moment, at the beginning of all time to come: ancestor to myself, *Homo habilis,* dusted in the gorge at Olduvai. Heat had desiccated those first forms of life. But Olduvai itself would disintegrate on impact with the ranges of Vermont. Ice is more terrible than heat, and it is against ice that future forms must pit themselves. Body numbed, it is the mind which decides to live. Or to give up and die.

But until it occurs, there is no way of knowing which choice the mind will make; and, sometimes, it is not until catastrophe that we know we must make a choice at all.

Thus numbed, I was not yet alive, thawed out, when first I heard black poets sing. Somewhere, cryogenically preserved, the dreams were there. But the dreams were no longer flickering, with movement calling attention to themselves. Stilled by inexorable cataclysm, the dreams were ignored: the dream had died.

I was not alone, a solitary individual pillared by the freezing blasts which came, suddenly, as the inner doors were opened to our national life. There were many of us rooted to the impervious permafrost. There was a road there, somewhere; but we did not know, we did not care. As a species, strengthless, we were about to become extinct. An age of ice had come again, covering, layer upon layer, the interlocking brick.

We are nearing forty now, those of us who were the children of The War. They have many names for us, pejorative categories in which we seem to fit. We are called "The Silent Generation,"

"The Safe Generation," "conformist as army worms." One of our own writers, Pete Hamill, says: "We had forgotten how to feel because it was too dangerous."

"He goes seeking liberty, which is so dear, as he knows who for it renounces life."

They had killed us with their wars of liberty. And their wars had eventually brought death to the dream; had made stalagmites of the roots of verdant Oz: petrifying freedom, turning us all to stone.

I no longer heard the howling wind. I no longer heard anything. Through the long decade I had listened as successive reels of film unwound themselves, year after year, through my viewing machine. Protest dulled. There was too much of it: too much hate; too many promises eviscerated, left to decay; too many murders, too many deaths. There were too many dangers there. And thus I wrapped the film and track around myself like a celluloid winding sheet. Mummified by the end of the decade, I watched and listened. But I did not see and hear.

Boredom, I am told, is a symptom of anxiety. Perhaps. But I had become very bored. I was a film researcher. I had a painful, tedious job: plowing through thousands of feet of news film, searching for an event, a phrase, a segment from someone else's life. Most of what is there has never reached the screen. It has been expurgated, cut, made to conform with the requirements of time. But I had to find unfamiliar scenes which the producer could snip out and insert, like jagged pieces, into the jigsaw scenes of the documentary film which must explain, must synthesize, must highlight event. And if all our events were varieties of war, what I must find were the visceral motions of those wars: I must fill their Movieola screens with beatings, with blood, with a visual catalog of our violent acts. "Never let history interfere with a good story," a producer had once said to me: if it fits, we print. Everyone has something to say. They say it . . . endlessly. My hands work the manual rewinds automatically. I no longer have to listen to every word. All the whining sounds the same. Turn the reels a little faster: the voice of Donald Duck. So what? Save time. There is money to be made, lots of money to be made.

I have a reputation for a squirrel skill: the visual instincts of the well-nourished Hollywood child. I have no idea why I tab scenes the way I do. It just happens that way. I do not think about it. Evidently I satisfy, for in this overpaid industry my free-lance fees run one hundred dollars per day for my nonexclusive time; and if by the end of the decade my work means nothing to me anymore, I am compensated for it by the series of restless amusements this cornucopia of riches can buy.

There were some consolations to the company to which, finally, I attached myself, giving up freedom for security and promises. They were visionary men: we would do great things; and meanwhile, high purpose still ruled our professional lives. We were film makers to the young; educators, really, using the most affecting tool of our technology, washing young minds in imagery. Thus we plundered the massive archives of the Sherman Grinberg Film Libraries in New York, whose clammy vaults contained much of the filmed history of twentieth-century man: old Paramount newsreels taken by America's star cameramen, some of whom died to bring us the truth: Damien Parer on Pacific shores.

(Clark Gable sets up a scene with toy planes and indigenous personnel on a China battlefield many years ago, when I was just a little girl. In Chicago, someone sets a match to a picket sign and the camera films reality symbols we have made.)

Paramount News, now stored in vaults, is disintegrating fast. There is no money to transfer it to safety film. Nitrate history crumbles under viewing machines, turning to dust. I had patiently sat through many of these as a child, as our brave boys launched still another attack and jackbooted Nazis thrust their legs up and across the screen: sinewed steel, hardened by the blitzkrieged march across the European continent. The tracks they made were omnipotent. It was a dance of death: frightening, macabre, studded . . . beautiful.

Stored at Grinberg, too, was the current product of the ABC Network news team, who poured thousands of feet of brilliant color into the Library each week. All film could be purchased for reproduction. Network news has time only for a brief scene here and there to keep its viewers interested.

Black history was my job that winter after our triumph on the moon. We appreciated the commercial possibilities of a series for their children, who would now study themselves as they did the people of Mexico and Japan. I had been watching black for ten long years. I was sick of viewing the same scenes again. Still, it would sell. But what would the framework of such a series be: what was a theme that we could sell? "Go out and see what you can find. Here is a list of names," the producers said.

Obedient, loyal, grateful for peace, I took the list. I selected, listened and made notes, searching for the theme, a cohesive direction upon which to build our success. Black? Okay, if you must. But black what?

It was only another series, one of many I had done: "Churchill," "Truman," CBS's "Twentieth Century," NBC's "Project 20," "Battleline," "Survival." That's all it was. But far below my feet, unnoticed, there was a tremor in the glacial continent. In the beginning of all time, I did not feel the movement yet.

To be fair, we have decided to give voice to the living proponent of an historic confusion. Watching Eldridge Cleaver in the small screen of the hand viewer, I notice, first, his eyes. They are lidded heavily, and wisps of smoke haze the colors on the screen. He singsongs his belief. I am convinced he's stoned.

"You have an organized conspiracy going on in this country composed of right-wing reactionary racist demagogues in conjunction with the police-military-industrial complex: avaricious businessmen-exploiters."

I remember the dialectic sophistries from my youth. In grammar school, the class communist exhorted us to May Day's parade. Her auburn pigtails held in place by rubber bands, she ignored the prettiness of our bows; ignored the beauty of our land. We knew even then that she was wrong, for we had heard differently for many years, seated in the picture show. Between the horrors of Frankenstein and the heroism of Errol Flynn, there was Henry Morgenthau, selling War Bonds.

"This is a war of life and death. On our side, springtime, and the fragrant smell of new-turned earth. On their side, the stench

20

of decay and corruption and smoldering ruins that once were homes."

Our country protected us, and if there was organized conspiracy, it operated to conspire against our enemies who would make our lives a ruin. Warm, comforting, our father nation made us safe and we could rest, sheltering, as we did on those long prewar weekend afternoons, in the woven blue-print hammocks, rocking gently to and fro; as I heard the stories of the Marne, pennons flying over magic kingdoms named Château-Thierry and Belleau Wood, which, in later days, somehow got intertwined with Birnam Wood and witches' tales.

In later years, the class communist wore rubber bands, but then we wore starchy little bows that stood straight up on our brushed and shining heads; or were plaited within the long and silken braids to end in formal balance, bits of ribboned color on each side of a bubbling face.

We waited. The long twilight of Friday afternoons hung behind us, above mountains and the well-tended lawns. It seeped between the trees, crept to the porch. We waited. Starched and dressed, careful not to muss ourselves, we were like a bobbing bouquet of cherished young American flowers: pinks and whites and yellows and blues, we bounced up and down as we hopped impatiently on sturdy, well-browned little legs, our dresses like tutu petals about to burst.

Around the curve in the mountain, beyond the white-painted, bracketed hotel, floating through the twilight air, the whistle sounded its notes: the train arrived, shooting cinders into the warm summer breeze. We heard. The bouncing increased.

Behind us, rocking on the porch, the mothers sat, hands folded quietly, talking softly, slim silk dresses gracing their mothering protective forms.

"The child says . . ."

"My husband does . . ."

We hopped and played and talked ourselves: "Is your daddy coming too?"

"Do you think it will be hot?"

"When summer ends and school begins . . ."

21

"Are you in kindergarten yet? I'm in first grade, first grade, first grade. . . ."

"Do you think that we will fight?"

We did not listen to their talk. It was not interesting. In various sizes, mixed with little boys in knickers or well-ironed short pants and sturdy shoes, we waited impatiently on the wide, gray-painted wooden porch. It was a special time, was Friday night, and we had come running in from streams and fields, fingers and tongues blueberry-stained, to get ready, to get washed and scrubbed, to get dressed, to become again ladies and gentlemen, princesses and princes, instead of young, free animals. They would not find us as we were, devoid of ceremony, for it was—for us—a cherished ceremonial time. The daddies were coming; and as the hot, tired, dusty men arrived in a parade of hotel limousines, we would rush, flying off the steps, and be swept up in their strong, male, sheltering arms.

"Kinder, kinder," he would call to me. "My Jujunu." To him, I suppose—we never talked of it, we never had the time, he died —it was reward in full; reward enough for the hot weekday city nights, for the greasy restaurants, for being all alone while his family was protected from the heat, the child from dreaded polio. No matter what reward they would deny him for a quarter century of work down at the Navy Yard *(Juden Verboten!),* here he was given, unquestioningly, all there was. Here there was uninhibited joy. Here there was unrestricted love, knocking his silver-frame glasses off with a thousand kisses planted on his nose. He was precious to us, precious especially during this very brief weekend time. For soon he would have to return: duty-filled, honor-bound. And he would explain it to me at other times, seated on the upper deck of the ferryboat, during the moments when we passed Liberty; telling me over and over the verysame tale (I never tired of hearing it) of when he was a little boy and saw her greeting, promising him.

This was the last summer. That it was soon to end forever; that the twilight would soon change to smoking gray; that storms would forever rip at the dream . . . that it was soon to end forever, we could not know. It would have ended anyway, in nature's course, for children grow and in parturition sunder themselves. But nature was also gathering itself for another death, in periodic challenge to our lives.

Across the sea, a little boy was playing in a mountain field. His father did not come to visit on Friday night. His father, mounted on a juggernaut, was crossing the Russian steppe, the one my father had left forty years before. We did not know each other then, or know that someday we would meet. We had to become enemies first. "You do not understand the ironies of war," today he says. No, I do not. How can I love my enemy?

But if, on these last Friday nights, we dressed for my father's return to us, we created of that return an event out of proportion to the rest of the uncaring world. They had returns of their own, on other mountains, amid other coasts. What did we care? We three, we loved. We: family. And to my mother and myself the love was deep and quiet for this gentle man with the iron sense of privilege for his new nationality; for the freedom to challenge he had bought for me. He talked little of his own escape from death. He never mentioned the word "pogrom." I suppose he thought I would never need to know such things. He carried no signs. He waved no flags. But he was what America was. In the summer of 1941, America was him: the immigrant in the last of the peaceful years when we had only love to glorify and had not yet learned to love—and glorify—hatred too.

In winter, in the front parlor, lined with deep, plushed blue chairs, waxed furniture and lace curtains which hung still behind the closed and sparkling windows of my grandmother's house, we sat together, my Daddy and me, and listened to music on the radio while he read to me Prince Valiant tales.

"Ladies and gentlemen," the urgent voice suddenly said; and, in future days, my father sat, head bowed, *Life* Magazine diagrams open on his knees, mourning, as one by one his ships went down into the freezing, prehistoric sea. The *Arizona* was the first he lost. (It was the first on which he'd worked after long years of engineering school at night.) And later, when I saw the films of

23

it, effects mixed in studio, I could not tell whose screams it was I heard as the waters closed. Was it the sailors, clawing at the shattered, impervious steel; or was it my father's inner voice, locked within a mind embolized by tragedy? It did not matter. Like them, he was doomed; like his nation, doomed, he was still to live a little while, fighting for many years while he drew plans and plans and plans to keep us safe, to fight this war and the one after that. He would save us, my mother and me. He would save the world in his own way, who had known glass shattering in the night when he was young; who had seen the phalanxed mob and heard the roaring animal voice; who had smelled the charring fires as stumped bodies burned within the ruins; who had looked up somewhere, sometime, to see the narrowed eyes which, sightless, did not see the little boy. Reviled, less than human, less even than the animals who performed some useful task; no nation would protect his life, no flag was his to cherish and protect, except for the one he saw, finally, from the deck of a crowded, filthy boat: the flag the class communist exhorted us to ignore, now Cleaver says, "to preserve democracy in Babylon."

Stoned: hallucinating from some bitter, twisted dream where the cannabial poisons loose the uninhibited, primitive response. Reality drops away; and Cleaver would involve me in his nightmare of hate.

But I know who the enemy is. I have known for a very long time, though now he has another name. The lessons I learned still apply. If there is hatred in America, it is the hatred born on that early December day.

There is hatred in America, now Cleaver says. Mindless, his images are reversed. But there is hatred in America; and it is hatred I encounter at the end of the sixties in the world of film: black faces turned, twisted with rage as I, defenseless, dead, without the armaments of life, sit watching as they pull me into their roiling, unexpurgated world.

Split-screened America, images askew, unwinding on the fossilized road. They have declared war on me. Surprised, I do not know it yet. Nor do I know, for the voices are still whispering and hard to hear, all that I will be called to sacrifice.

There is hatred in America; and, in America, there is again to be a total war. The price of liberty is very dear. That is a lesson that I learned too.

ℳ 3

The mind of man seems to need lines of demarcation, reference points along which we can sight in order to define where—and who—and what we are.

We draw our maps in a variety of ways, sketching boundaries which sometimes overlap, sometimes converge at one point to then scatter in a shellburst of unconfined direction: which sometimes do not meet at all. Thus each of us uses the reference of others. We do not only define who and where and what we are. The reference of others gives us a means of judging ourselves qualitatively too.

Time is divided as well; and we mark off our ages collectively as a species, individually as each of us grows from infancy to old age. The definitions are exact, give or take ten or ten thousand years. Carbon dating reduces error when we deal with materials such as timber and stone and fossil bones. But there is no machine or scientific instrument which we can use to correct the errors in separating the ages through which each of us lives. Adolescence ends with the twentieth year of life; and middle age begins somewhere in the fifth decade. But the criteria by which we tell ourselves where we are are made flexible by the very organisms which define. Life span lengthens. Will middle age someday begin at fifty-five, or sixty-five? Boundaries change. Will the Common Market someday itself evolve into definitions which eliminate structures of territory? Where will our categories come from then? Where do they really come from now? Do we really know that exact moment when some genetic combustion occurred to set the primitive primate on the road to developed man? Do we really know that exact point in time in ourselves when the first recombination occurred within the emotional synapses of our minds to evolve us out of adolescence and into developed maturity?

We look back over time and say, "It happened then." We have tools for this, the electrical charges of memory. We flick a switch, the light goes on, the reels begin to turn and, viewing, we look back and see the image of what we were moving under our eyes on a screen.

But when it occurs we are not photographing ourselves; or, with instant replay, in slow motion defining each action of our lives, to say: "This is where I began to lose. This is where I began to win. This is where I first put my foot onto the road which has led to now."

Some roads are well defined and welcoming. We enter willingly, certain of our happiness to be journeying there. And some roads, though also well defined, we follow most reluctantly. We journey there only because we must, because there is no other way.

One day, in the last months of the old decade, I seat myself again on a high metal stool before a viewing machine, to continue the dulling journey I must take into the world of black.

I have seen Cleaver and dismissed him from my mind. I know he's wrong. But here is Dick Gregory, uncoiling on my small viewing screen. Dick Gregory, a funny man. I welcome him. I am always a comic's gourmet and so, winding slowly so as not to miss a word, I have a sense of cultivated delectation, waiting for the feast of laughter, a few moments of humor before the speechifyin' begin, as Amos—or Andy—would say; would also say, "Hello dere, Sapphire." We make a joke of it, lowering our voices in imitation of black—itself caricature—while my mother bustles from stove to sink to kitchen table.

"Hello dere, Sapphire," we laugh and play, pushing our toy carriages on concrete afternoons, rocking our porcelain-skinned, well-dressed dolls, while adults, seated on the slatted folding chairs, complain, "The *schvartze* didn't come today."

"She didn't come? So you're surprised?"

"Be grateful," chimes in a third. "When she comes she doesn't steal?"

We heard the silent obeisance made to God. In our homes, we knew, neither did the *schvartze* drink. There was no liquor there. Drinking was for *schvartzes* and the *goyim*. They were people poor in spirit, not like us: the chosen ones, following God's ways and thus triumphing over mortality. It was a demanding discipline asked of us and cleanliness was its outer form.

"The *schvartze* didn't come today." Down on their knees, the mothers scrubbed. The *schvartze* was off somewhere, probably in a factory. In time of war, it was bodies which our nation needed. We would sacrifice ourselves, to put another piece of hoarded waste on the assembly line.

But if the *schvartze* did not come that day, the humor of that distant world penetrated all of America; and we listened as we ate, wordless at our evening meal, only the noise of Amos 'n' Andy on the radio and our chuckling sounds as we chewed away.

But time evolves, and I am here now listening again willingly to Dick Gregory. Though he is a different sort of comic, I know, still he has always amused and entertained. I will have a few laughs in the middle of this assignment which will be, I am certain, deadly dull. I am so very tired of all of this.

Gregory's face flickers on the small hand screen.

"People," he says, "whether we like it or not are controlled by nature. If you put a tight shoe on your feet, you get a corn. If you wear the shoe long enough it turns into a callus. If you wear the shoe long enough it turns into a bunion. Eventually it'll wear the shoe out.

"Black folks in America got a callus round their soul and if the system don't back up, their shoe is going to be wore out!"

Amos and Raggedy Andy flapping their soles on Harlem streets.

Skip to another routine, a more serious bit of business here.

". . . A free man is a man with no fears, and when white folks fear me marrying their daughter eating in their restaurants going to their schools living in their neighborhood, he is my slave by the law of nature whether he like it or not."

Freedom from fear is America's code. In the land of the brave all men are free.

But Gregory continues to lecture me.

"Revolution is nothing more but evolution. Evolution is a gradual naturistic change. It leads into revolution, which is quick change. . . . When you get nine months pregnant nature don't care if you married or not because that's not one of her laws to get pregnant. She don't care if you have Blue Cross Blue Shield. . . . When a woman gets pregnant, the first nine months is nothing more than evolution, which is gradual change. When the water bag break, that's revolution, which is that change and all the soldiers on the face of this earth couldn't cross one woman's leg when the water bag break and keep that baby in."

Behind him there is a too vivid screen whose pattern I cannot make out. Under the lights, Gregory's close-up black head begins to sweat. His opening pores infect my mind.

"Nature's law is when you are nine months pregnant she is going to drop this baby,"

into the camp where children are sent,

". . . if it means death to the mother and the child."

I shiver. In black and white, flashes of concentration begin. Gregory does not let up. There is no mercy. Anywhere.

"America's racial pregnancy is nine months pregnant. . . . And we got a right, a right to hate you the same forward way you hate us!"

I have seen what hatred does; and now begin to see again soldiers marching through the reels.

"America is the number one racist country on the face of this earth . . . and if we don't make massive changes, this country is doomed!"

Racist America? We are doomed? That is not true. For it is we who had given life to those whom racists had condemned; who had rescued the numbers with our arms. Like the dead girl in camp two summers after the end of war. She was a Pole from Maidanek: with stretched white skin, a broken nose and a frizz of uncut, dull blond hair which surrounded her face like tangled lint. She had escaped, but not alive, and silently thrust out her arm for us to see the small blue numbers among the veins. I knew nothing else of her. I remember nothing else, for she had no incident among us; she did not get involved as we shouted and cheered and fought our way through color wars; and paired up to exchange silent kisses in the dark with senior boys; and made our beds sprung-quarter tight; and led our horses through blue-ribbon maneuvers in the ring; and exhausted our bodies in the pool gasping for the lifesaving badge. There was Chuck (whom I loved) and Saul (who loved me) and Marie (who was loved by Chuck) and Roseanne and Jerry (who were content). There were dozens of others whom I can see, faces flickering, around the campfire at night during honor ceremonies when the crafts counselor, dabbed with paint, came shrieking down the hill carrying a torch, circling the fire as we stood solemnly waiting for his touch, which would push us out from the ring and make us members of the secret, cherished order that meant we were better than all the rest: a child's elite society.

The Pole stood with us around the fire but, never picked, never noticed, we did not know that she was there. I worked hard for my selection, curbed my natural truant ways, shouted and demanded my reward. The Pole said nothing. I do not even remember her name or anything about her except for the day she thrust the numbers on her arm at us. We looked at them. We looked away. We ran off to swimming time.

But I knew then what the numbers meant, for I had heard them whispering in the dark hours of my family. We did not yet—two summers after the war—say those names aloud. My father could not say the names at all: Auschwitz, Belsen and Dachau. Something terrible had happened there. Jews had died. A mass pogrom. But death was only a phone call in the night: Grandpa

Trotsky, Grandma Trotsky, Grandpa Lauterstein. Death was only a funeral for the very old, too sick to live. Death was only sitting on a box for a week, while visitors brought dried fruit and nuts. That was what death was: only some hidden going-away, a process I could never understand, for those who went away were only glimpses to me of bent huddled creatures rocking silently against their pain. It had nothing to do with who I was. In the center of the universe, I stood on sturdy, muscled legs. If dea'h came, I would run away . . . faster than the fastest wind. (I was a champion at that and won every camp prize there was.)

Besides, I had something else. For I was an American child, and I also knew by then, for I had been taught for many years, that no one would ever write numbers on my arm. They would not dare. If I knew what death was, I knew as well just why I was, and always would be, protected and secure. For there were heroes in America who would give up their lives for me, raising a fist and dying proud as Cagney did sitting in the cellar of the SS torture room, calling down a rain of bombs upon his head before pain made him betray our cause. He was a suicide in all our names, earning honor, living forever in the minds and hearts of countrymen: a posthumous, technicolor life, like Colin Kelly, whose colorfoto picture I had, at the beginning of the war, carefully cut from the *Daily News* Sunday magazine and pasted on the door to my room along with a dozen pictures, close up and far away, of the flag that all our precious boys were dying for; and in the streets we played Nazis and Americans on the empty lot, crawling through untended weeds with rifles made out of twisted sticks; and echoing machine guns' noise with high-pitched gurgles in our throats.

"Eheheheheh! I got you. You're dead. Fall down."

Crumpling grotesquely to the ground as, in the movies, I had often seen it done, I lay there silently, my wounds invisible to grown-up eyes. Dead. Dying. Bleeding to death. It was my turn. I did not protest; but then, by some unvoiced process of our childhood fantasy, would resurrect myself to change my side and shoot my twisted twig and scream, "Die, die, you Jap, you dirty Jap!" For we could cross oceans at will, change sides, die and be reborn, puncture and reheal ourselves; over and over again, day after day until dinnertime, until our mothers, shouting from building windows all up and down the block, demanded we return from war. "You come into supper immediately or I'll break your head!"

Unless, of course, there was no game that day, for there were other duties to which our childhoods were called by the nation to whom we were so lucky to belong: America which allowed our wars to be only childhood games. Only games, not reality.

In the newsreels we heard them speak, like Ambassador Joseph Grew, after Pearl Harbor, returned from Japan:

". . . I have had ample evidence of the work of these barbarous hordes, seizing, bombing, burning, bayoneting and then, when masters, raping, torturing. . . . I know the Japanese military machine, that ruthless, cruel, utterly brutal machine which, like the juggernaut, is riding roughshod over hitherto peaceful lands. . . .

"Today the lands and people of East Asia; tomorrow, the lands and people of our own America. . . ."

We would survive. We had to fight. In fevered cadres they sent us out, a battalion of children across the land. In Hammond, Indiana, the Junior Emergency Employment Personnel Service washes windows, tends the young. (Mother must work in factories.) In Washington and Boston and Hollywood and Hempstead the children worked: throwing rubber on a pile; rolling tires like toy hoops down streets to toss them on waste pyramids. It was unpatriotic to save money: buy stamps, buy bonds. It was unpatriotic not to save everything else: we saved, we sought, pulling wagons we scoured buildings, burrowed in basements shadowed and damp. Hauling and dragging, we collected things: tons of paper for our cause; old shoes for frozen children's feet; tins of every shape and size upon which we jumped with all our weight; bits of soap and hoarded grease.

Because I was a girl, I trained in the domestic arts by sitting at my mother's side. She taught me to roll the olive wool skeins from around a chair; to knit one, purl two; to bind off the long, imperfect scarves. We would send them with our love to some unknown boy, flinging his body at the hordes. My mother also taught me to sew, to stitch bits of flannel into tiny robes for infants whose parents had disappeared. Busily my fingers worked, training female dexterity. We rolled bandages, rolled them tight: boxes of bandages to cover spurting wounds and bodies whose flesh hung in threads.

Some general's face looms on the screen. Which movie did we see that day? I cannot remember which it was. The double bill changed twice a week.

"You must have the fighting spirit," exhorting, he inspired us. "If you call that hating our enemies, then you must hate them with every fiber of your being. You must lust for battle; you must scheme night and day to kill."

Who will be the Jap today? Not me. Today it's your turn to die.

"There need be no pangs of conscience, for our enemies have lighted the way to faster, surer and crueler killing. They are past masters. You must hurry to catch up to them if you are to survive. The sooner you get in the mood, the better and more skillful you shall be when the real test comes."

Like children of all mankind's tribes, we trained ourselves in arts of war: in the weeds we marched and shot. And in the weeds prepared to die.

"The struggle is for survival. Kill or be killed."

In school we learned our lessons well. It's a drill. It's a drill. How fast can you empty the halls? Or should we huddle, arms over heads, underneath the ink-stained desks? Do not speak. Don't say a word. The Nazis come. They'll find you there.

At night, sound blasted into my pink-walled room; the sirens wailing, rising and falling above the city battlements like the witch's manic screams. Under the bed I clutched the amulet, the plastic disk with name, address and date of birth, so they would know who I had been if they found me buried there. And in the dark, turned my face as I had been taught, away from the window glass, to protect myself against the bombs which would come any minute now, borne by evil monsters in dark squadrons flapping their wings.

"Lights out! Lights out!" the warden shouted from the yard.

33

"Turn the goddamn lights out. Don't you know that we're at war?"

Turn your lights out, please, turn them out. The Germans, howling, ride juggernauts in the sky. I hate the Germans. I hate the Japs. They are the enemy. Turn out the light. They will drop their bombs on us like they did on all those other places we saw on the movie screen and then they will come in, boots marching in the night, plundering our land. And us.

We are Americans, the savior land.

On another day, the President, our father, speaks:

Grant us honor for our dead who died in the faith,
Honor for our living who work and strive for the faith. . . .
Grant us brotherhood, not only for this day but for all our
years. . . .
We are all of us children of earth. . . .
If our brothers are oppressed,
then we are oppressed.
If they hunger,
we hunger.
If their freedom is taken away,
our freedom is not secure.

We are Americans! We save the world. We fight. We die. They shall not win. "Kill or be killed," the general said.

We learned to fall in love with death. Oppression existed in every time; and on my wall, inside the room, behind the Colin Kelly door, were pasted pictures of Gene Kelly: D'Artagnan, who had, later, come swashbuckling into my life, leaping with great shouts of joy into contests of the sword; who would fight courageously, sworn to do so to the end; who sent me immediately to the library to take out every book on his life. I read them all, seeing, every time I saw D'Artagnan's name, Gene Kelly's face upon the screen. For they were one and the music of *Romeo and Juliet* would become for me forever the music describing love as D'Artagnan held his dying bride, never never to care again once she was gone.

Love was tragedy whose real dramas we could only feel if

34

parting was a final form, the most romantic love of all: to be a tragic figure to the world, to love, to lose in tragedy; remembered forever; the lovers die their deaths for us.

In love, someone has to die. Thus death and love are intertwined; and I the tragic bride well loved; or my lover D'Artagnan, whom I could not live without, for, dying, he would leave me helpless, undefended and alone, at the mercy of the Japs.

We loved, we died. We paid the price. We sacrificed our well-loved young. The vegetable man's son was missing over Germany. I had not seen him for many years: a tall, strapping, red-faced blond with burly arms hauling packaged brown bags into our house. Missing. We presume he's dead. I did not remember him very well, but after the telegram came to his parents in their clean, verdant little store on Rutland Road, he became more real to me than when he was there; for his plump, red-cheeked parents who had been, before, part of a whole complex of neighborhood; who had, before, selected good things to eat with love for us, their customers ("The melons? They not good yet. You wait a week or two. They better then.") . . . his parents now carried their flesh around, taking coupons, making change. Their aprons grew soiled. And in the window, her head raised above the pyramids of fruit, their dark-haired daughter peered out at our busy shopping street. Her eyes did not move as we hurried back and forth, buying aspirin on the corner, milk at the store farther down the block, crossing the street to spend a nickel after school in the candy or the pickle store. Motionless, she stared straight ahead until, after a while, we ceased to notice her and her eyes became part of the display; two random black-purple grapes just lying there: waxed fruit. We heard rumors, whispers from the adult world. She never, afterward, said another word. Finally they had to put her away.

One terrible winter, when Christmas came, we heard other whispers from the adult world. Surrounded! A Nazi counter-offensive had begun. Encircled, our defenders fought: the panzered tanks rolled through the snow; at Malmédy a massacre, the blood of innocence shed vengefully. Surrender? They would rather die. "Nuts!" the American general said. We held our breaths. We prayed for them. And prayed, as well, for ourselves too. Was the cause lost for which the vegetable man's son died? Would the tanks come rolling here? I was afraid. Could we lose? And if we did, what would happen to me: bayoneted on a German lance?

The breakout occurred and then the inexorable armies swept through the ravaged, decaying world: in pincered movements carrying vengeance everywhere. Springtime came to Europe again, but splintered trees do not bloom. Through forest, over untended field, the armies rolled: shelling, grenading, shooting flame as, one by one, the barbarian homes were cauterized.

The charred earth could bear no more. Once Hitler had done a dance. Now his haggard generals met, slowly signing the last of their cards. We won. We won. V-E Day came. We danced in the lot where we had played. The game was not over. There was more. But for now it is enough to shake our childish arms and raise our fists in victory. We had not died.

The super's wife would not dance with us. In their ground-floor window a banner hung. Love was gone. And in its place there was a star which had, somehow, turned itself from blue to gold. "My wife, she feels no joy in this," the super said. After the war they went away.

We had lost the father who had sheltered us: my mother cried at the radio. I was in the movies that afternoon. But, mourning, still we carried on. "Two down, one to go!" we said. "On to Japan!" we cried.

A few blocks away an aunt went to work, came home and cooked and cleaned and took care of my aged grandmother. She was grim-faced all the time. Her son, my eldest cousin, sent letters home: "Somewhere in the Pacific," he said; and later I was to learn that he was on Iwo in those days. It would cost one million American lives, we heard, to take their island from the Japs. My aunt did not know exactly where he was. But she trembled at thinking where he would have to go; and her pain, like waves of shock, traveled through my family.

A new kind of bomb, the radio commentator said. I cannot now remember his exact words; but I remember where I was on that August day, sitting at the white-painted table in the rented house in Hurleyville; and I remember the feeling on the small-town streets in midsummer, 1945. Everything was still, suspended, nothing moved. I went out back to tend the violets I had grown, pulling up the threatening weeds; and into the attic of our house to sit in the cool and musty shade, poring over old copies of *Liberty* magazine, to see the pictures of other times, long ago, before I was born.

Nothing moved. My father rarely came. Sometimes we would go into the middle of the town and count the railway cars, shrouded with tarps, reaching for some important, secret port. One day we counted one hundred as they passed. Once we saw tanks, real tanks, like in the movies, and were pridefully impressed at their deadliness. To be inside a tank, to sight through slits, to shoot, to kill, to drive spiked tracks over the enemy form. To hear them crunch and scream and plead.

At night we rocked upon the porch. We waited. Nothing moved. The country town was hot and airless. I do not remember that we ever swam. We waited, silent, for the word.

It came. Our upstairs neighbor was shouting on the stairs; crying, laughing, she thundered down. "It's over. The war is over. The Japs gave up!"

Is it over? Is it real? Switch on the radio. All over town the switches turned.

"Ladies and gentlemen . . ."

We danced, manic now; we danced, frenzied, unafraid. All the lights went on again. There'd be no sirens in the night. The war was over, danger gone. In Times Square sailors kissed the girls.

Hitler was dead, burnt in Berlin.

Soldiers climbed lampposts, waving flags.

Mussolini long-hung by his heels in an Italian square, his mistress upside down with him, skirts over disfigured head. Clara Petacci; I remember her name.

America had saved us, saved us from death. "Kill or be killed," the general said. And when, long afterward, I saw the Hiroshima films and the Nagasaki victims, skins in shreds, bodies blasted into shadow on concrete walls, I could not really care at all. Kill or be killed.

It was their death; their death or mine.

But Gregory would call that racist too, a holocaust of yellow skins. Do I explain barbarian hordes? Dick Gregory lived through those years. Definitions differ in different times. But some things no one can ever explain.

One day we stopped playing. One day we stopped gathering tin. At the end of the field, on the ground in front of an apartment court, a crowd had gathered, horrified.

"What's happened? What's happened?" We ran to see.

Crouching, we peeked through grown-up legs and saw a lump of sheet-covered white, soaking rapidly with spreading blood. There was a neighbor lady there, splattered to death on hard concrete. She was not alone under the sheet. She had thrown out her baby first.

They never explained those deaths to us: the murder and the suicide.

And now I sit upon the stool, wounds unseen by other eyes. Racist America? We are doomed?

Dick Gregory shoots his twisted words and yells die, die at me as hurriedly I wind the film. I have selected enough to print. Gregory goes back to the vault. The comic has somewhere lost his art. He is not funny anymore.

4

I am, for some reason, wandering erratically in the beginning of the alphabetized list: ignoring *A* for Abernathy and *B* where it applies to Edward Brooke. Selecting first from verbal wars, in this way I come to James Baldwin, to whom I listen carefully. I have never read any of his books. Neither have I heard him speak before; and, though his reels are very long, they absorb me fully for many hours.

There is, however, an odd sibilance on Baldwin's track; as if, somewhere, a slight breeze is playing within the microphone. But I tab his speeches anyway. Perhaps the technicians and their sophisticated machines can, with some mysterious electronic gadgetry, fix on the distortion and find a way to wipe it out. If not, still the producers should listen to what Baldwin has to say. His words are very meaningful: a reel of poetic reasoning that will add a knowledge we must have.

And then, thoughtfully, I continue my wanderings among other angry men, listening to the sharp rise and fall of voices on my tracks. Why is it, I wonder, speculating idly, that all rages seem to be centered here? If your name starts with *B* or *C,* do your teachers automatically seat you up front where you are ever under their watchful eye and not allowed to twist or squirm or whisper or be a little child doing the things that children do? Especially if your skin is black and you have funny, kinky hair? Thwack! Be still. Shut up. Pay attention. Do not speak. Sharp rulers cut across the tender, soft-child hands. Silence or pain.

Hush, child. Don't answer white folks back. Don't anger them.

And if—like me—your name comes at the end, and they seat you in backroom rows where no one notices or calls on you? Is that better? Do you, after a while, hold all your childish answers back, swallowing your fierce little-animal energies? If no one cares, what happens then? If no one listens, does that mean that what you have to say is meaningless: you do not count? Are you invisible to all those cherished people who scatter their gold-paper stars like symbols of their love; who appoint the class monitors to rule, relegating you forever to powerlessness? So that, in the end, the proofs of your nonexistence accumulate; lie rooted in the interstices of your mind where, in the end, they bring uncontested fulfillment of their prophecies.

Stokely Carmichael brings some answer to my questionings, I discover, unreeling him through sprocket wheels. "We have got to unbrainwash ourselves," he says. I find him standing under the lights of the Tougaloo College stage; and, though I can first appreciate the blocks of fact he uses as prologue for his text, it is what he builds on them—and how—in which I hear and see a menace that somehow disturbs.

Viewing, I find his introductory conclusions inescapable. Surprised, I adjust the earphones and fiddle with the magnetic head, centering it exactly on the track. It is important that every word be clear. I never thought of this before.

"The biggest lie that this country has told about us is that we are lazy. *We* are lazy?" sarcastically he catechizes them. Under television's lights, the young faces turn in rapt attention as Stokely injects his young audience with the tenets of the new self-belief.

"White people are so lazy they sold us to do her work for her because *they* was too lazy to do it."

Delighted, the audience smiles and nods.

40

"You run up and down this highway, run up and down the Delta, visit southwest Mississippi. We are the ones who are out in the hot sun picking and chopping cotton for two dollars a day, while they're sitting on the porch.

"While *they're* sitting on the porch!"

The audience cheer and raise their fists. Right on, they shout. Right on, again.

"If the history of this country were written, you would have to say that this country is a nation of . . . thieves." He comes down hard on the word.

"If I said to you that Christopher Columbus discovered America, you would say that's correct. But now, here comes this honky from Spain. There are already nonwhite people here and they're not existent until they come and discover them. Ain't that something?

"Ain't that something!"

Something is wrong with reasoning here. It is the same sort of twisted illogic, I think, that he has, with much justice, so vehemently exposed in us. But, voice rising, Carmichael rips off other myths.

"All the heroes have been white. They make you bow down to George Washington as your hero. Did they ever tell you that honky owned slaves?

"Yeah! Not only did he own slaves but he sold a black woman for a barrel-of-molasses. Our hero.

"Yeah!"

The speaker works on: body warming with the effort, sweat begins to soak through the cloth of his well-cut yellow shirt. His lean form moves gracefully as, with each paragraph, Stokely Carmichael changes roles.

"Instead of our black leaders, instead of our black leaders having the strength to tell the honky, 'Later,' they begin to react to his definition: that he would say, 'Oh, no, no, no, we don't want to marry your daughter. . . .'"

The actor in another time steps 'n' fetches down the stage.

" 'We don't want to be your brother-in-law. We just want to be your brother.

" 'We don't want to sleep in your bedroom. We just want . . .' "

The audience laughs. They always do. But Stokely's switch clicks on again.

"So that what white America was able to do was to have us react to her definition. . . . And we never got anywhere because we were playing her game.

"Now in Snick, when they asked us that question about whether or not we want to marry their daughters, we tell them:

"—your daughter!

"—your sister!

"—your . . . Momma!

"We tell them:

"Yes.

"Yes.

"Yes!"

The audience applauds and cheers as Carmichael produces act after act. Skillfully the rhythms of his speech rise and fall and rise again, each time to greater height as he bellows his audience into flame. He is a master of the technique. Heartsick, I wonder where he learned; for, with a mounting, arm-waving peroration, he ignites waiting elements in Tougaloo's hall.

"The total white America," he shouts, "the total community is incapable of condemning herself for the acts of brutality and bestiality that she's heaped upon the total black community.

"She can—not—do it."

Thundering black fury, "America," he screams, "cannot tell the truth about herself. If she did, she would have to commit . . . suicide!"

Dramatically, he pauses. Mastered, the crowd awaits his word. Then, seeming for the first time to recognize what he has said, the leader smiles his curtain line.

"That might not be such a bad idea," he says softly: an afterthought.

The sea of young black faces jump from their seats. Agreed. They cheer. Death to all whites! The leader speaks. Death to our enemies.

Watching, my terrible recall burns its own images; the nightmare flickers at my mind. In black and white, the scenes repeat: eliminate the alien race. Should we let such swaying hatreds speak? In World War II America, Leni Reifenstahl's extraordinary film trumpeting the *Triumph of the Will* was banned. Its genius was too subtle and overpowering for the ordinary mind. And long after the war, when I was already grown, I too had witnessed the power of its images and sound: "Horst Wessel," the Te Deum to another god, as the strong young bodies tossed the liturgies of all civilized history upon the flame; as a thousand torches formed pinpoints of light; as puissant banners filled the screen; as eagles glowed from every spike.

The lords of war were gathered there. Soon they'd ride into the night. In plated steel they'd carry death. But now they sit with close-cropped heads turned to the stage. The camera pans. They're all alike: waiting for the Niebelung.

And there he stands, the haloed figure immersed in light. A thousand throats proclaim their joy. He stands and waits. The young men shout. He calls for death. They stand. They cheer. We are the master race, he screams. They roar defiance at the world. The Fatherland will rule the earth.

I saw the film. I understood.

I understood . . . nothing at all.

For, one day, when I was still young; one day in the early-morning hours at the beginning of the week; one day I saw the intercuts: the extended history of Nuremberg. Journeying to the Army's archive in my little black German car—the "people's wagon" a Jew had bought—I sat before the viewing machines, while the rotund Army dwarfs burrowed in the vaults, bringing up reel after thousand-foot reel prepared as evidence at the trial; never fully released to movie news. They were a collection of the German record, the Nazi's self-annotated history; the history precisely documented by the Reich so that, a thousand years from now, the descendants of the new order could unearth them, as we now unearth the glories that once were Greece, and marvel at the chalked towers of great monuments. When one builds a monument does one recognize that one is mad? Is monument-building a manifestation of insanity? Madness, insanity: the words do not fit. But what is the word for what happened there? Still, today, I do not understand. Or, I am only beginning to.

From the first frame of film, threaded in the large screen of the Army's viewing machine, I knew why what we had seen between features on our movie screens had been so cut. It was nine in the morning and, after that first thought, I did not think anymore. I could have stopped watching. I needed only a few hundred feet to make the television editor's point. I did not stop. I finished one reel, arms exhausted by the heavy film dragged through the tightened sprocket wheels. Then I threaded another, wound, viewed, finished and began again with the third and then the fourth. I saw them all. There was no time. People passed around me, I am sure. They must have. They did on other days.

But not now. I was not there. I was crouched behind an old ragged man who wore a high dusted black felt hat and a grimy overcoat, his white curled beard like a shirt front of hair over the threadbare lapels. I had a cap. My eyes were large. He had one arm half behind him, holding me.

"Achtung Juden!"

Who are these men? They are very tall and blond and their eyes are like bits of blue glass, like ceremonial goblets fallen from the tables of feast to shatter on the floor.

I do not understand their words. Does anybody know what they mean? It is a language never heard before. *"Achtung Juden!"* Do not speak.

> When you grow a little older,
> when you grow a little bolder,

says my mother as she rocks me in her arms.

> When I was sick and lay a-bed,
> I had two pillows at my head,
> And all my toys beside my lay
> To keep me happy all the day.

44

She brought me juice and fruit and books. The doctor came with medicine. Was it measles, chicken pox or mumps? It did not matter. I was safe. And lying in my Brooklyn bed, I could arrange the covers as I willed:

> And sometimes for an hour or so
> I watched my leaden soldiers go
> With different uniforms and drills,
> Among the bed-clothes, through the hills.

They waited for the fever to break, for spots or scabs or lumps to disappear. I did not care. I played and played: I moved my armies, fired my guns.

> I was the giant great and still
> That sits upon the pillow-hill
> And sees before him, dale and plain,
> The pleasant land of counterpane.

They gathered us with bayonets, with roars from a cage of animals. We did not speak. The words were strange. We clustered, sheltering, while around us grew the ring of steel. Down cobbled streets we began our odyssey; among the ancient, wet-mossed buildings silently we went, as through a canyon at the bottom of the world whose towering sides peeled off striations of time and met, somewhere, high overhead; so high there was no sunlight reaching us.

We did not speak. The shutters above the street were closed, bolted by iron latches from within.

Where are we going? the little child asks. Be still, the adults whisper back. Make no noise. Don't anger them.

I want to play. I want to eat. I want to go to the bathroom. Be still. *Verboten. Du bist ein Jude.*

I see you there on the screen. Gentle, puzzled child—the Pole —they put the numbers on your arm. Did you ever cry aloud? Did you ever cry again? And what of that young girl trailing you? I see her portrait, too, on the screen . . . afterward. They have put

45

her under the photographers' lights, breasts bared, to witness the experiment; and then, naked, marched her off.

Who spoke? Who cried? Who shouted rage? Silent, obedient, we marched in line, thrusting out our pale-skinned arms while needles punched numbers in the pores.

But what are numbers on an arm? We are all numbered in some way; and if our tattoos are made visible, so what of that? Symbols of slavery do not make us slaves.

But what is this? What is *this*? No living thing ties women's legs. They must come from some other world, some monstrosity grown in arid space, mutanized by a retching, unnatural catastrophe.

The young, grimed, clean Americans come in, vomiting; herding before them a plumped, drawn civilian populace which did not know the camps were there. The Germans load the carts, flinging the sticks with bulging eyes and swollen genitals about. Today they do not bother to be neat. There is nothing to be constructed here. Later they will build again: we send them grain, our treasury. Soon we will return their film. Now they must clear the rubbled ground away.

> When you live a little longer,
> when you grow a little stronger.

And, later still, stronger and now grown, I watched the scene in the spring garden of the outdoor cabaret as the young, sweet voices rose in Hollywood's dramatic synthesis of what had been: as, one by one, the bodies stood. Under the budding, flowered trees they sang, offering themselves to the consumptive flame as Germany would rise once more; and on the screen, and in my seat, an old man and I turned quickly gray. Only we, perhaps, knew what it meant. Sobbing, I watched; sobbing again. It was only very recently. In the plush theater, I was the only one who cried aloud.

But I had not yet seen Hollywood's film when Carmichael punched the combination that sent the reels of fear spinning on replay, like a machine which will never stop again: a perpetual pendulum which, with every pre-timed arc, slices deeper at my life: when, under the lights, Carmichael first ripped off the scabrous skin.

Where had he learned this technique? An ancient tool, an ancient response: the young blacks cheer: they'd murder me.

Carmichael calls for my death. I have no voice to protect myself. How could I fight them anyhow: gentle, fragile child trembling silently, faced once again with biblical plague?

I want to run. I want to play. Now grown: find peace; with forgetfulness find camouflage. Run away, running wild: run to a forest in Vermont. The poles of me have been magnetized. I crash upon a mountaintop.

The invitation comes just in time. I need to be among my own again; and, this weekend, I have been invited to an elaborate leisure chalet. I will be warm and comfortable. Relieved, I push away my fear. I will be safe for a little while, toasting myself with community.

It is Saturday night: dinnertime. And so, drink in hand, I gather with the others under a burnished copper lamp around a mahogany table covered with mats of finest cloth. Outside, a cliché moon gleams on the forest of black pine. Thermopane walls mirror flames which roar in a monumental hearth whose perfectly fitted stones rise, like a tower, high into the eaves.

We are, this weekend, a chosen twelve, apostles of the American will. But hovering unseen, there are also others gathered here; for silently Stokely has followed my track and James Baldwin has found it too. Converging, they are getting very close, threatening an extension of themselves. Their acid reality melts every wall. I will never be alone again.

On my left, the Kings Point graduate sits. He has been cast by Hollywood, I am sure: tall, broad-shouldered, weathered by the sea. They have written him a role of tragic irony. He is a rising officer in our disintegrating merchant fleet. It is no longer Columbia who rules the waves.

"Lazy," he mutters, fingering the goblet of European wine with which we are rewarded for this perfect day. "They're all lazy."

Autonomous switches click on the internal projector I carry

with me. Remote from my control, Stokely unreels, in living color, the passions of his dialogue. "The biggest lie that this country has told about us is that we are lazy. . . ."

Unaware, I become his voice. Turning to the officer, quietly I say, "You don't really believe that."

Not believe? Of course he believes. Most certainly believes. His glass tilts dangerously toward the table around which, in casual, sporting luxury, we have gathered for our evening meal. Above us, flickers of light lick at the A-framed roof.

James Baldwin cuts from the shadows. Unbidden, nevertheless I cannot ignore the sudden flare as he forces himself onto the split screen of my interior world.

"The youngest country, we like to say; the richest country, we like to say; and the strongest country, we like to say. And yet the very notion of change, real change, throws all Americans into a panic. And they promptly look for another label to get rid of this."

The experienced officer counters with dialogue of his own. "They just don't want to work." His deck hands defy; commands fail in execution; career and fleet's at stake. He produces his episodes while we wait. Behind us, in the kitchen, a bank of electric devices times a perfection of feasts for our delight.

Stokely's speakers blast away, raging through the cacophony of tracks. "*We* are lazy?" Venomous at the motherland, emotion reveals a destruction of syntax. "White people are so lazy they sold us to do her work for her because *they* was too lazy to do it."

Around the table, the warmth of mutual agreement links the guests. Abstractions of race are only a discussion still. But Baldwin's portrait is etched on nitrate stock.

"A country built on dissent . . . now debates with the individual in as many ways as it can because it has placed something above him: safety and security and money." New Horsemen ride. "And when these things are cultivated in a country, when these things are honored in a country, the country, no matter what other things it may have, is in danger of perishing.

"No country can survive. No country can survive!"

But I know I have survived because of this country; and this country has infected me with belief in its technicolored dream.

48

An immigrant boy has kept me from the ditches of Babi Yar. He paid the price nevertheless: admission to the dream was overwork: a civil servant's coronary in midspeech before a pride of admirals. It was a fitting, American death. But before he died, he brought me safely to the wilderness, and armed me well. God had promised him a new nation. His promises to me are now kept. But what I do not yet understand is that—alone—I have been following a mirage, and have wandered dangerously close to an alien land.

Inexorably, Baldwin whirs on. "The problem is the price. Not the price I will pay, but the price the country will pay. The price a white man and a white woman will have to pay in themselves before they can look at me as though I was simply another human being.

"This metamorphosis is what we are really striving for. . . ."

Why spoil all this? I have everything now. I am a member of a special breed. Experts all, our American inheritance has given us immunity from gravity's law. In perfect form, we can lock our skis and fly across the snow; revel in the crisp, cold sun; and chase each other like a flock of plumaged gulls down the steep and shining mountain. And when the vanishing sun makes the light dangerously flat, we board a caravan of cars whose special steeled transmissions carry us easily up through ruts of unpaved private roads; and within our terminus we sip our drinks and slather pulverized goose livers on Danish thins that look like bite-sized matzohs. They are scattered freely in great handfuls on a teakwood serving plank. Picture-book people, we are gathered here in celebration of the rites of achievement. It is the Après Ski: the order I am entering blazed upon my consciousness.

There is a harsh new wind in this alien land. "They're talking about us being lazy!" Stokely screams. "We are the ones who are out in the hot sun picking and chopping cotton for two dollars a day, while they're sitting on the porch."

Relaxed now by the wine and warmth, the company has gathered at the table, a frieze of faces against the paneled walls. In the kitchen, the buzzer rings. The bird is cooked.

49

Carmichael repeats: "While *they're* sitting on the porch!"

Long skirts sweeping over hard-planked floors, our hostess enters rolling a brass cart on which are set translucent china plates. The turkey is perfectly browned; its skin crackles, like crisped parchment. The conversation continues. The officer is a most attractive man.

"But you don't understand." I smile at him. "They're not lazy. It's the only way you've given them of fighting back."

"Fighting back?" An absurd idea. Too ignorant for tactics such as these. Everybody knows. They're all alike. The lady of the house, wife of a rising industrialist, inserts her scenes: don't trust any of them, they'll lie to you every time. "Let them in somewhere and . . ."

The mayoral aide, liberal's appointee, contributes too, as do the corps of educators seated there. Do we all not know? We have at least one degree apiece. Some of us have two—and three.

Stokely must be wrong: "The total white America . . . is incapable of condemning herself for the acts of brutality and bestiality she's heaped upon the total black community."

Carmichael does not understand such things. Truth, I know, will always prevail. Am I not, though in great danger, questing after truth? It is the American way. I cannot deny what I have begun to learn. The illogic of innate assumptions offends the proud rationality of my educated mind; and so I produce facts in evidence before this jury of my peers. "We've all been brought up with these ideas for so long that we just accept them without thinking. Put yourself in their place. How would you react if people hated you just because of what you were born?"

"When one has emptied one's heart of all human feeling, you would do anything to anybody and justify it." But it was to the Germans that Baldwin, there, referred. The Germans, certainly; not us.

Rank attacked, the officer is vehement now, the courtly naval manner gone. "They bring it on themselves. They're just not capable of following the rules. They're animals. . . . Their cabins stink."

At the table, all concur. But I cannot. I am from peasants bred.

50

". . . one of the simplest ways to lose your freedom is to stop fighting for it. . . ."

The tablets of justice are melting here, incinerated by a white-hot rage. Released, Baldwin's demon dances to a manic end.

"If I have found out.

if I have found out,

in spite of all that you have done,

that I am not

a nigger

and I know that you invented him

because you

needed him,

then it is a very big question:

Who is the nigger here?"

Beside herself, our hostess rises, flinging waxen shards into the furnace of obliterating hate. "What makes *you* such an authority?" The door clangs shut.

Is there another word behind the crackle of the flame?

I am not prepared for that. Carmichael has frightened me; and now, with candent fusion, they raise terrifying blisters on my skin.

It is no use. I am alone. I do not dare answer them. Remembering, I subside. For the rest of the weekend I am . . . tolerated, silently. Among these twelve, I am Judas: invited to the feast, betrayal printed in my genes. And, like Judas, it is silver that has brought me here. The real price is yet to be paid. And I am the one who will pay it.

"That might not be such a bad idea," Carmichael says. The young blacks cheer. Death to all whites.

But fires change pigments in the skin. What color have I now become?

5

It is now time to do battle with H. Rap Brown; a confrontation I have been trying to avoid. I am excoriated by what I have so far seen; abraded further by the weekend in Vermont. Unanswered black, unanswering white forces dialogues back within myself. I am isolated, alone. But my angry fantasies build great soliloquies upon the screen: with intercuts I chop them up: filmic psychodrama tripping pain: celluloid Rorschach unblotting memories I do not wish to have.

Unanswered black, unanswering white: reeling forward in a laocoön swirl of film, they threaten to punch holes in me and push me off into a contending, dangerous universe.

I am commanded to uproot myself, but I will not go quietly. I am a civilized human being, and thus long past self-destructive states.

"Man in a state of nature is man against himself." I remember the words from riots at Columbia University. I am the evolutionary product of five thousand years of learning, of commandments to be good. Be still. The evolution has been gradual, a "naturistic change." It is not wise to be so angry. It is not wise to lose control. Bombs burst in brownstones on West Eleventh

Street. Anger brings down the walls: young bodies die. I cannot care for human torches that chose to set themselves on fire. They have made time bombs of themselves. But now, raging, I have become a time bomb too.

And now, under the magnifying mirrors which flash black light at me, Rap Brown becomes the fuse.

"The question has been raised about why black men fight and have fought for this country. It is the black man's implacable will to be free that makes him fight *for* this country. And it is that same will that will make him *fight* this country."

He is seated at a table, facing the color camera's eye. Behind him there is a clutch of sycophants, one of whom wears the image of Marcus Garvey embossed on his soiled shirt. He thrusts his chest out for us to see: Garvey, where black power's voice first was heard: Garvey, the con man, the exiled thief.

"How can you tell people to be nonviolent and at the same time condone the sending of white killers into the black community?

"How can you say that you are for peace when in the same breath you condemn one war and condone another?"

His voice is sneering, contemptuous. I return his dislike. I have long since passed judgment on this man. His attitudes are pathological. There is something wrong in his twisted mind.

"I say violence is necessary."

Not here. Not true.

"Violence is part of America's culture. It is as American as cherry pie. America taught black people to be violent. We learned well from America . . ."

The revolutionary criminal's excuse. Cop out.

". . . so if we accept any of your culture at this point it will be your violent nature. . . ."

I am docile, quiet, still: pinned by stone tablets to the law.

"Each time a black church is bombed or burnt, that is violence in our streets.

"Each time a black body is found in the swamps of Mississippi and Alabama, that is violence in our land.

"Each time black rights workers cannot be protected by the government, that is anarchy.

53

"Each time a police officer shoots and kills a black teen-ager, that is urban crime."

Twisted, turned around. Excuses to rob, to riot and to kill. Death to the whites. The enemy.

"Individuals do not, remember, create rebellions . . ."

They use them for their own ends instead.

". . . conditions do. Until they begin to address themselves to those conditions, rebellions will continue. And they will escalate. . . .

"You see, we recognize America for what it is: the Fourth Reich. And we tell America to be on notice, because if white folks is going to play Nazis,

"black folks ain't going to play Jews!"

Jews? Jews! He is saying that to *me*? Fury uncontrolled, I wish to smash the glass of that machine. What kind of Reich is it you are living in, Rap Brown, that turns its cameras on you and lets you defecate your hatreds in front of fifty million nightly viewers? Ask Jesse Owens what the Reich was really like.

It is America that kept you safe. How would you fare in Hitlerland? I know how. I am America's child. Alive because of it. And you are too. Love is the rule defending us:

> "If our brothers are oppressed,
> then we are oppressed. . . ."

On our side there is springtime, the seeds of life. You shoot your twisted words at us. Die, die, you say. I am a gentle American child. But I wish your assassin well. Your hatred makes me want to kill.

I swallow it. I do not speak. It is un-American to hate like that. I punch buttons on the library phone. "I can't stand it anymore."

"You're too involved," the producer says. "Take a few days off and go away."

To find myself within another group; sitting, strangely exhausted, in Sugarbush. There is a haven here, on the second floor of the Valley House. Below, a mass of skiers jams the facility, floors trembling under the clomp of rigid boots accompanied by the discordant spurlike ring of buckles. Pushing in never-ending procession through the doors of the lodge, they form themselves in dense, snaking lines behind the wooden barriers leading to the lifts: above and below me I see them, packed like lemmings volunteering for mountain cliffs.

We will now have to wait overlong in order to ski, for I have been late in arriving this morning. One of the passengers assigned to my car complains: victim of my lassitude.

From the group of strangers, a kind face looks out at me, guttural German accents gentled by an Austrian birth. The little boy in mountain fields, now grown, smiles and proffers a verbal hand. His tone is soft, his voice is warm.

"You must learn to get yourself in order," gently he says.

"Order is for peasants," I spit at him. "Nobody orders me around!"

Shocked, he recoils and turns away to join the stream of skiers reaching for the top. I am shocked too. There was . . . hatred in my voice. In me? Hatred is a weakness of the primitive mind. It is criminal. Uncivilized. It is Rap Brown. Enjoined from such feelings, I thrust them down. But hate is what this feeling is. Where is such a terrible thing coming from?

Staring out the window, above the skiers who move steadily within the twisting barricades; staring down, fighting for control, suddenly the iron latch breaks. Unaccountably, I burst into tears. I am ashamed. I cannot stop.

Overwrought. But by what?

There is a break in the walls somewhere, breached with a catapult propelled by rage. Why? I do not know. No matter. I must ski. Stand up and shuffle into the cold, heading straight for Castlerock. My yellow goggles half cover my face. No one can see the tears which freeze in streaks, crossing the plastic panes.

The mountain is most terrifying here. Jagged hillocks march down the slope; twisting, curving, they do not stop. The trail is narrow, sharply banked, lipped by cliffs whose only barriers are hardwood trees. They'd break a fall. They'd break me too. I am alone on Castlerock. No one will come and rescue me.

It is deadly to ski here today: a glistening blue glaze covers the slope. But I will cling with edges of knife steel and slice at valleys between the mounds. Their peaks rise high above my head; my skis screech on the boilerplate. I lock my legs. I turn. I fall and slide, crashing, out of control. I try again. Sweating, I must get away. There is a howling overhead. I must escape. I plant my pole.

"Animals and slaves are named after and by their masters. Men name themselves," sneers Rap Brown.

I am a Jew, *Juden, achtung, verboten.* They are coming to get me in the night. Into the oven goes the Pole.

Unseen in the crystaled forest trees, shadowed black faces hide and watch. The sound of cheers howls like the wind. Unseen in the valley they're watching me. Unseen they watch me challenge death.

The silent Pole thrusts out her arm. They dig their ditches at Babi Yar. The machine guns sound, ahead of us. But still we march forward (on slippered feet), shuffling forward in ragged robes.

"... if you are going to play Nazis, black folks ain't going to play Jews!"

Jews? Jews! You are saying that to me? Rap Brown, I will burn your effigy and, childlike, dance around the flames.

I thrust my ski pole into ice. With linked S-turns I overcome. A Russian's roulette played out in the snow. The odds are bad. They fill my need. The haloed figure stands in light. I plant the spike tip very deep: imprisoned in the frozen earth. The leather strap pulls off my wrist, wrenching my arm with a stab of pain: the saber shimmers in the snow. It vibrates like a tuning fork, faster than the eye can see; its movements against the icy air generate an encasement of heat. The ski pole glows and turns to red. Great cracks appear in glaciered ice.

The funnel lengthens. It grows dark. The end is somewhere still ahead. I will not hate. It's not allowed. Child of America, crashing down an American range.

It is very late. I come to rest, finally, between the papier-mâché gondola and the Gate House Lodge. The lines are gone. All the lifts have stopped. The Austrian is coming down the hill, his heavy expert skis—like unbending beams—carried easily on one

56

shoulder. He uses his poles for walking sticks.

With his head he motions to the top of the hill, to the Valley House. "They wait for you up there again," he says.

Stepping out of my skis, I say, "It's my car. They'll have to wait."

He chuckles and shakes his head. "Yes, it is your car," he says and, still smiling, continues down the road; walking comfortably in his rigid, still buckled boots.

It is the last day of the decade. The lifts have stopped. Night comes to the mountain. All the cars are gone. It is very quiet here: the gondola bubbles hang motionless, growing dark and shapeless in the freezing silent air.

It is the end of the decade. We are the last to leave, traveling back over the roads, headlights picking up the mounds of splattered, oil-flecked snow: sleepy in the warming air of the purring automobile.

It is the end of the decade; and, ending it, I stand in the white oblonged-metal shower and turn my face to the cascade of steaming water which opens and cleanses the skin; feeling the force of a dozen pinpointed streams on the muscles of my neck and back: heat penetrating, easing the ache I feel.

It is the end of the decade: a time for celebration: a time to dress myself in silvered turtleneck and white belled pants: a time to sit, drained and quietly alone, before the fire in the simple shabby living room of this new club which I might join. We are housed within a farmhouse south of Sugarbush, whose added wings seem like an unplanned afterthought. The barewood floors do not meet. There are empty rooms whose doors stay closed.

Stairwells are shadowed, secretive, as if they were meant to be hidden behind some tapestry. The kitchen is vast, with long counters and huge black iron stoves. And in the dining room, long tables abut each other to form a U.

In the den, a room much smaller than all the rest, there is a stone fireplace, a bar, a few worn and overstuffed armchairs and a gray threadbare carpet covering the floor.

Still, I am comfortable here and, thoughtless, bake myself while *Gemütlichkeit* vibrates and voices sing and bottles pour and foreign languages mix with misplaced English verbs.

A new year is flying in and I can hear it overhead. Its beat is a gentle fluttering in the room. The sound is peaceful, rhythmical.

The club is ordered, well arranged. A hutmaster is in charge of everything. This weekend it is the Austrian, I learn. It is his duty to pour the champagne; and, as the others form a circle in the dining room, holding out their paper cups, he quietly passes from one to the next, filling each. He does not drink.

And, as midnight comes and the members begin to celebrate, he stands in the doorway between dining room and den, watching as they drink and laugh; as the boys each grab a girl; as undirected polkas end in bumping, colliding hilarity.

The Austrian does not join in. He watches as, with mimicked passion, everyone kisses everyone else: mouths meeting for an instant and then mouths quickly pulled away.

In a corner of the den, I am watching him, watching the three-quarter face and the easy, comfortable body that lounges against the doorway gracefully. He is wearing a simple sweater of some soft, thin wool and a pair of well-cut pants. The sweater is beige, the pants a loden green. They fit but do not cling. There is a fine subtlety about his dress. It reveals nothing and still reveals, to an x-ray inner eye, the dancer's form that must be within.

Yet, in the doorway, he is unmoving, very still, like an exhibit in the Natural History Museum. Only his eyes seem to be alive, flickering over everything; restless, watching, as the paper hats tilt and bob. His eyes are strange, half-lidded over cheekbones that protrude. There is obviously some genetic mixture here, I think, as my mind strains back to remember which tribes swept into his country, conquering it, long ago.

There is a conversation at the bar, a Swiss reaching for the proper English word. Turning automatically, I tell him what it is. I have not spoken much. Surprised, he looks at me and then asks for definitions, for the rules of placement, which I do not know. The Swiss teases me. "English here is very bad. You ask why this, why that. They do not know."

The Austrian appears, suddenly, it seems. He has come to

agree. "Always they break the rules," he says; and then listens, concentrates, as earnestly I explain why some languages live and others die. And, at the end of my lecture, offers me a drink, going behind the bar to prepare it for me, coming back to stand with me, though there are others there; and then, after a while, to offer me his arm and lead me into the center of the den. It is growing late. The others have wandered off to bed. I stand waiting as he changes records in the phonograph. It clicks, the plastic disc drops down. The music has a familiar sound, but I have not danced this way before.

The pressure of his hand in the small of my back is slight; but still he guides me firmly as we swirl around the room. Smiling, he watches my face as if to see its expression; as if to question and contemplate whether I will follow where he leads.

Looking up, looking beyond the cheekbones, past the curve of bone and taut, pale skin, I create a catwalk above us strung with lights; spots of blue and gold and red swing in arcs, meet and melt and follow us. A thousand candles flicker on the strung-crystal chandeliers; the floor is marble, polished smooth; ancestral paintings hang on every wall; the walls themselves are covered with a silken brocade.

The camera whirs. Gracefully, I hold my gown. Tall and glowing, the short one-shouldered cape of his uniform sways as we dip and turn and whirl around the room. The courtiers all have left the ball. The orchestra plays for us alone. And when they too leave, slipping silently out with the last hours of the night, the Austrian extinguishes the candles one by one by some magic that only he knows; and, standing, holding me in front of open windows through which come the fresh breezes of a new decade, he whispers in my ear.

"You are so tame now," he says; and then, pointing out the pinkening sky, he says, "Ah, see. It is only a little adventure we have had." Holding me, together we welcome this new year; together we begin adventure there; holding me within his arms under the candles whose wisps of smoke linger upon a sound of gently beating rhythmed wings; holding me in the cove of his arms, he says, "You are so tame now," and I find, as I listen to his

59

voice, that something has gone. "What do you mean?" I turn, to raise my face, to look into the strange, uptilted eyes.

"What do you mean?"

But all he says is "We cannot stay here like this. It is against the rules to get involved." And, leading me away, holding my hand, we mount the darkened stair where, leaning over me again, he says, "Come. It is time to get some sleep."

And, resting my arm upon his, he escorts me through the narrow corridor; careful that I should not trip upon the ragged runners whose threads are treacherous in the dark. Bowing slightly, he leads me to my door and then, turning quickly, melts away.

It is five in the morning of January 1, 1970. Outside, the sun has just begun to rise over the untracked fields.

In the quiet farmhouse, I cannot hear; but a blast of trumpets begins to sound. In the quiet farmhouse, I cannot know.

January 1, 1970: in America, a new age has begun.

Book Two

Generations of Silence

✇ 1

Nineteen seventy: a new decade. The Baldwin reels have been refused. Unusable, they are rejected and returned. And though, above the wind song in the microphone, the poet's voice rings with a clarity that sets the crystallized ganglia quivering, the poet's voice must be ignored. Production values are paramount. Baldwin is restacked: buried again within the vault. The children will never hear the *nachtmusik* of his prophecy.

But I do. I listen again and again. The lyric litany repeats in my mind, note after note: a bolero of truth: the background score of every scene.

I am very tired now. But I cannot forget his words:

"In order to be free you have to look at some facts, facts of your
  life, very hard.

"You have to look into you and know what you are
and what you are not,
and decide what you want
and take it from there."

Nineteen seventy, a new decade. We are not what we knew we

were. But for what we are there is no name. What will the scientists say of us? Are we mutants who will quickly die? Or are we the first of a new survival form?

"People are free . . . as they wish to become. If one sees all Americans in this way, it begins to be a very sinister matter, the way freedom is used here.

"Freedom is used here mainly . . . as a synonym for comfort.

"People think they are free because they don't have a military machine oppressing them. And they overlook the fact that one of the simplest ways to lose their freedom is to stop fighting for it."

How shall we fight? For what? For whom? We have forgotten how to feel. Who will give us feeling back? A miasma of cynical disbelief fogs colors of our furled, unmoving flag.

"I still believe that when one has emptied one's heart
of all human feeling,
you would do
anything
to anybody
and justify it."

We all have numbers on our arms. A federal prescription embalms us all. In built-in sarcophagi we rest from pain.

"A country built on dissent . . . now debates with the individual in as many ways as it can because it has placed something above him:
Safety
and security
and money."

But we have been wounded in an ancient war. We need time to heal, to renew ourselves: to find out what we were and how we became what it seems that now we are. But, looking back, trying to decide what I will be, what I see is that I am still on a journey that I began more than twenty years before.

". . . it is your country.
And your responsibility

64

to your country is
to free it."

I knew. But I knew these things too when, sweet sixteen, when, one day, I stood in a marbled cathedraled hall and lived the scene described for me:

"Grand Central Station: crossroads of a million private lives. Gigantic stage on which are played a thousand dramas daily."

It was not great drama we enacted there, the three of us: my parents talking, instructing, anxious-proud; while I, surrounded by possessions, awaited the train impatiently; and then, quietly, careful that I should not see their tears, the two of them let me go; and stood behind the barrier gate while, ever a child, their only child skipped down the platform away from them ... for the first time and the last. I was free. Free at last. Free to become, to find out what it was that I was, as an American, meant to be. But we were never to be a family again.

Slowly, gathering itself, the train pulled out of its tomb, striking sparks as it rumbled through the underground: a steel minotaur following the tracks, carrying me off from infancy.

Encased, rocked on prickly plush seats with little white napkins doilied on top, I journeyed—as the young have always done —to the west: to a new adventure: to life: to learn. To a passage that would never end.

There were many of us on this odyssey; crossing the flat night-plains whose guides were darkly weathered stakes strung with endless wires which buzzed and hummed above our heads. It was an aural autobahn, present in a horizontal web, as below the train bockets past, the sound of wheels like cadenced steps; rocketing through the countryside; crossing crossings; speeding past dead local stops whose lights were long since out; past low-slung buildings with flickering neon signs which had, a few hours before, and would, in a few hours to come, beckon travelers to umber hotcakes and coffee from giant chromium urns, to hamburgers on blackened grills.

We passed tiny boxlike homes whose shades were drawn against the engine beam which swept like a shaft in front of us, cutting through the peaceful night. The nation slept, fitfully perhaps; thrashing about in nightmares of the Red Menace at times; dimly aware of symbolized injustice, like a dark dream let out of the sleeping subconscious to enter quiescent, unguarded minds for a moment only, then to be reabsorbed, to disappear, to be swallowed up. To be denied.

The nation slept, exhausted by the burdens of our own self-forged arsenal. And raised its young men, the boys my age, and fed them well so they grew strong. We were in another war, but it was not here, was not declared. No richly timbred voice exhorted us from speakers in quiet living rooms, over the sound of Sunday papers being turned. We could rest. Go on our way. Toss out a can, a bit of soap, if that was what we chose to do.

Across the nation, on our coasts, great ships swung their cranes and monstrous rope sacks to lift huge cartons carrying food, medicine, machinery. Europe was being rebuilt. There are, again, guns: a police action in Asia; in the Near East, rumblings of religious war.

The country slept. America, having saved liberty for mankind, would do so easily again. Secure in our beds, sure of ourselves. Why worry? Turn over and have another dream.

Beneath the arch of trees (in a few years to be cut down, victim of Dutch elm disease) the mammoth complex of federally styled buildings consumed and disgorged us with semiannual regularity. In spring, our white-bucked feet polished and brushed, we carried our books underneath the green-gothic beams of trees. In winter, protected by fur-lined boots, we made paths across the stretch of fields. We journeyed to class bracing our young bodies against the midwest storms that traveled straight across the leveled plain.

In our rooms we sat at desks piled high with books; reading, memorizing, taking notes. Late in the night, we took our graduation-gift typewriters down into soundproofed basement recreation rooms to write the blizzard of papers heaped on us. (Seventeen in one term.) Assignments were long. They were due on time. Black marks for lateness, penalties against an *A*. We studied part of every day, on every night throughout the week.

But there was time, then, for everything; for we were very young and sleep was something not particularly necessary in our lives. The switchboard buttons glowed constantly. In our rooms a buzzer signaled us: three shorts, a long. We dropped our papers and our books and went racing, hair set above calamined adolescent skins, down hallways to the phones. He called. He called! Bursting into classmates' rooms, we did a little dance of joy. "I'm in love." Again. So am I. Me too. Did you get a lavaliere? Will you get his pin? And when? Does he love you, do you love him or him or him? You know, what's his name? The boy you met last Saturday.

Strung on cork bulletin boards were our growing collection of felt-covered bids: from freshman to senior years, we cherished every one, every bit of memory, every dried-out flower head, every gift from every dance. We cherished and kept them, long after the boys themselves were gone: some to other girls, some off into a distant world, some to the war that was the battle imposed on our youth who prepared themselves in ROTC. We did not talk much of it, or think of it, or rage at plans, engagements, marriages delayed. Widows perhaps before we were brides. Unprotesting, the boys simply marched off; as boys, unprotesting, always had done. And, one day, I went to a friend's room to call her out for a game of bridge. But she would not speak to me. Huddled under the covers, she waved me away; and, hushed, I turned and softly closed the door on her.

To have loved and lost like that.

On Saint Patrick's Day, one of my soldiers returned to school, bearing a carnation corsage tinted green, to pin on my proudly strapless gown: the layers of tulle over layers of lace my mother had sent me like a treasure in a tissued box.

They sent us chocolate kisses on Valentine's Day; and delivered hand-drafted cards.

> I love you love
> It is no crime.
> But I confess,
> I had no dime.

On certain nights, after the doors were closed, we could hear them softly marching, softly singing, coming in a long double line, rubber soles stealing down concrete paths, their songs as hushed as their steps. Someone was pinned. She wore a rose. And while she stood waiting in the window, above our well-mowed lawn, we raced to see the flickering candles carried carefully, lights glowing brighter as they twisted and curved around the walks. They're coming. They're coming here! The orchestrated male voices arrived, to quickly form themselves into a choral group, thrusting up their youthful baritones in the chants of chivalry: brothers forever, united in love:

> The girl of my dreams is the only girl
> Of all the girls I know—
> Each sweet caress like an angel's breath
> Cast in the after-glow . . .

Oh.

The tempos of our time were sweet, melodic, moving. It was the music which penetrated us; the music against which we closed our eyes to be swept away as we did on other nights when love was less legitimate. And we made forays to the littered streets where we were not supposed to go, to sit on hard chairs in ramshackle rooms, sucking up the sweet-smelling haze and listening while, in the almost dark, the sensitive braille fingers measured out portions of saxophone sadness to us all; and on the raised platform figures hunched swaying over their instruments; stood still and waited for the riffs of other minds; listening in on each other's midnight dreams. Jazz. We listened, the bass like staccato thumping, a wisp of drums sliding over stretched, taut skins. And rock, unbaptised yet; but to us a catalyst that made us bounce upon our seats and laugh at innuendo—we were so wise, so sophisticated then.

Our young faces were all that was white in that room. But we were not uncomfortable. We went in packs. We did not go alone. But we went often; hungering, now that I think back on it, for something beyond the glistening and ordered world that we knew then. For, I remember, we often wandered, too, over the back roads of Illinois, searching out grubby roadhouses where we could watch the Jukeses and the Kallikaks and dance to nickel phonographs pressed tight, so tight, and left to make love undisturbed as we barely danced in this forbidden territory.

It was a time of learning, a time to grow. Our violations were smilingly controlled. Caught breaking curfew, trying to climb into dormitory windows late at night, we were confined to the building after school for a week. And then, properly contrite, were free again.

We did not rage, protest. It was not unjust. (We found a way to circumvent alarms.)

In class, our rebellions were encouraged, cozened, allowed. And we could theorize on theories of relativity which some future genius, we proposed, might find could be overcome: and spaceships in that distant time might find a way to travel faster than the speed of light; to journey to galaxies other than ours and return in six months or a year and tell us all what was there beyond the stars: of strange creatures who were only particles of light, who existed only in each other's minds. The instructor smiled and disagreed. It could not be. He explained why it could not be. But we got our *A*'s for thinking too, for imagining, for suppositions which broke some rules and began with "What if . . ." For that was how all great discoveries were made, he said. We were the young minds, burning, growing, stretching; and it was our minds to which the nation would soon have to turn. And thus we were cherished, protected, guided—as all disciples are— and taught first what the rules were, though still allowed to test.

We were responsible children, they knew, and were given the freedom of responsibility; except, of course, for sex: one foot on the floor, supervised necking, no parking in the ill-lit underbrush.

We did not protest. We met the challenge, fought back in our own ways, secretly; and kept it hidden from them and from each other; and gossiped about the girl in the dorm whose mother had bought her black lace underwear.

In Journalism School they taught us how to write the news. And gave us our own daily paper to run, unsupervised. I had a distaste for the women's page, and so chose to cover the town police, who, obliging my request, locked me into a cell so I could see what it was like. (Our god was Hemingway: we must live in order to write.) They let me out very quickly. Panicked, I could not breathe; and, seeing my face, the portly town magistrate made a joke and gently changed the subject to the latest robbery.

It was part of our training to experiment, but still they watched out for us, for we were children still. And on election night, 1952, wrote us special passes so we could stay up until dawn and stand over the clattering wires of the AP machines and weep as the gifted poet of our age was defeated by a nation still expressing its gratitude for salvation from the war.

They did not think much of us, this outside world to which we would soon belong. We found out much later. As former Associate Justice Abe Fortas wrote in a little red book called *Concerning Dissent:* "Only a few years ago, in President Eisenhower's administration, many of us despaired because the college generation was so passive, so docile and so uninvolved. It was apparently uninterested in anything that was not safe, conventional, and serviceable in practical terms."

Like our nation, mirrors of our parents, we slept; not knowing that we did so. The needles of a decade before stuck in our skins, like invisible spines of memory. Our young systems, too young, too unprepared, carried an overload. The human organism practiced an ancient art: our bodies protected themselves. The Eisenhower Years, like a chronological stimulus to the A-Beta fibers within the mind, jammed all our circuits, making us unable to feel pain.

"People cannot live in a state of shock. Tired of a convulsive society, they settle for an authoritarian society." At the end of the next decade, in October 1969, the Vice-President describes that decade. But he also speaks our epilogue: an inscription for our youth. We had had too much noise, so we were still. Camouflage was necessary to survive, so we drew no attention to ourselves. We had our causes, but they were like the first combination of new elements. The unicell was still primitive, microscopic, unnoticed. We picketed barbershops which would not cut black

70

students' hair. (There was no TV coverage for our protest.) Our humor magazines were filled with satire: "The War We Do Not Want," an essay on World War III and on the red-devil-haunted foreign policy. (The magazine circulated on campus and nowhere else.) A Christmas issue advertised a novel gift: a Bigotry Set. "Make sure your child is the leader in his hate group." (There was no Archie Bunker then.)

From the Irish poet I received a flood of mail:

"Camp Kilmer is a staging area," he wrote. "During the war . . . everyone knew, after leaving Kilmer, they'd find themselves mixed up in one of history's bloodiest wars. . . . We were a war nation then, and we were turning out teen-age warriors. But everyone was a warrior of some sort. . . . And, of course, we all felt quite righteous about the war, and felt quite secure in the outcome of the whole thing. . . . We always knew we'd win.

"Would have been a hell of a shock if we hadn't. . . ."

In Korea, battles are fought. MacArthur is dismissed, contempt for authority too dangerous to allow. He wishes to chase the enemy into their own land, I learned, standing on the Journ School steps reading our paper's banner head. Our Army would be swallowed in the Asian waste. We would have to use . . .

We shivered at thoughts of holocaust. The enemy now had our bomb. And crossed the darkened campus one night, unable to talk, for we had seen a movie called *Five*, in which skeletons hung from crashed cars and on every street throughout the world there was only emptiness, and bits of paper scudded across concrete: the only movement left. For all was—and would be— forever still.

Ed Murrow attacks; Welch attacks. It's a different world. But always war.

"Kilmer is different than it was," the Irish poet writes. "The duty is a little dull. You pull KP, keep the area policed, pull guard. . . . All routine. . . ."

Stalin is dead.

"A liberal asks new questions," one day he writes. Trained at Kilmer, the poet is sent to Salzburg, into Teutonic Europe, questioning; and, from Europe, there are thick packets of mail:

71

"I feel combat." It is an Army expression, he says. "In civilian life we don't say it. What it means is if we don't get some indication soon that we've red blood in our veins, if we don't get a chance to swing at something or someone, if we don't go out and hang a good one on; if we don't get to run, jump, smash and scream; if we don't soon climb into bed with the hottest piece in Salzburg and make like two hogs wrestling in a gunnysack all night; if none of this happens we're going to apply for a Section Eight or go AWOL behind the Iron Curtain and bring out Stalin's body or Malenkov's scalp."

"I feel combat." We were all warriors then. These impulses were not so soon removed from us. Removed from America, placed within a film-remembered scene, the poet recalls, imagines, recreates what was once our childhood fantasy. "Die, die," we said and shot our sticks. But we were warrior children still, feelings of combat sleeping, but still there. We would take on the world. In our time. We were expected to: responsibility must be fulfilled.

My father wrote: "Our political situation abroad is getting no better very fast and nobody knows what strings are being pulled and what we are being led into, whether it will be war or peace. . . . I have had so much work fall on my department that we are swamped. The jobs are scheduled and we are two weeks behind on one ship already. It is supposed to have three months in the shipyard, yet jobs are scheduled to be completed in six weeks and we are two weeks behind. Or 33% in the hole. With all my experience in handling tight jobs, it seems that some things just cannot get done. . . ."

In America, "cannot" does not compute. We learned that lesson well in school. The University flooded our brains and then sent us out: "We the students of the Class . . ."

I could not attend the graduation ceremony. I was back in New York. My father had said:

"I worked as usual on Saturday. But Sunday, Mom and I left the house at 12 noon and returned 6:30 P.M. cold and nearly frozen. The house was so warm and cozy after the cold outside that we greatly appreciated the fact that we are free citizens in the good old U.S.A., privileged to enjoy the fruits of our labors and the kings and queens of our household. So long as we pay our rent promptly."

There was another price: on the seventeenth of March, Mr. Maurice Trotsky, who was addressing an audience of officers at the Brooklyn Navy Yard, suffered a coronary and fell dead on the stage.

"The first Seder is March 30," he had written. We had no Seder that year, or ever after again. "We have not seen you since the Christmas holidays." When I saw him next, he could not see me. Or any of the hundreds of others who attended on that day. My loner father, who had no time for friends or pleasures other than his work and family, lay in a simple coffin in the front of a large room where every seat was filled; where, along the walls, a solid line of blue stood at attention through a ceremony they could not understand, while gold stripes glittered in the afternoon.

I did not cry. I had no time to mourn. There was no time for death, no looking backward into fear. Out there the American heritage was waiting. It was promised us. My father's testament. Trained in belief: destiny is at the end of an upward road. To rise, work hard. Work hard; you will not fail. "Would have been a hell of a shock if we hadn't. . . ." But we had bought victory with our work, our dedication to the truths of flag. Work is the preservation of self from death: success is reward. It is written on the manifest.

For us, the American dream is reality. I have my degree; and take it with me on a six-month graduation tour of the lands we have saved. The Irish poet and I meet briefly in Salzburg, and then separate. He wishes to go to Greece, to stand among temples and suborn the gods. But I go wandering among other ruins; and, crossing the borders, napping at the sooted window of the train, am startled awake suddenly, searching for a place to run; for I have seen glimpses, from beneath half-closed eyes, of leather boots pounding on the station walk, and long overcoats flapping over knees; and heard the fearsome language once again. Run. But where? "Miss, your passport, please." It is green, embossed with eagles. There is no star. The train pulls out. I am still free;

to journey to Stuttgart and stand in the new-built hotel and over-look the shells of churches and decaying homes and know that I had collected tin and bits of soap and that I had helped to make all this. I was glad. And, after many months, I returned home once again, finished with wandering, ready to become part of the hallowed world. For I had conclusively proved to myself that there was no other nation, no other culture greater than ours. What good were paintings when they could be freighted away? Or great buildings, when they could burn, be blasted down? And the cuisines of Europe could become powdered milk and eggs, sent from our farms.

Childhood was ended. I had seen and learned and decided who I was and what I wanted to be. Content, certain that I would have all that America had promised me.

Somewhere, far to the south, there was a rumbling, unfamiliar noise. I heard it, but I could not distinguish the words. I had become busy with my American life; with becoming what I knew I was. And, at the end of the decade, I had given up newspapers and magazines. Impatient, I entered the glittering world of broadcasting to become, by 1960, participant in the greatest processes of man.

In the windowless room, surrounded by machines, I watched the images flood the now-tuned countryside as the keynote speaker measured out his words in time with our film. The great cameras focused, changed lenses, moved around. The control board, like the computered, metal-plated bridge of some monstrous ship, was dark; glowing only with lights from the monitors and the controls. We sat, watching the multipled images as the battle of the sixties was launched. The director's voice was like a low and constant hum: "Take two, get in a little closer, ready film, twenty seconds, switch to film, ready one, take one, closeup three, ready three. . . ."

We had stayed awake throughout the night, hunched over Movieolas, cutting the film they had sent me to find: the photographic paintings of our land: the American faces, concentrated and absorbed in work; the reapers in the field, harvesting our waving grain; the children playing freely, tiny legs reaching for the sky as they pushed their swings; the women, aproned, standing on the steps, drying their hands in the last hours of the day. We believed. This was the image of America, there; and, absorbed, fevered Americans ourselves, we worked inside our hotel room cage, visited by a procession of senators and congressmen who dropped in to see what we had done, to watch over our shoulders; while, next door, the Platform Committee sent fresh promises as each proposal was newly typed; and the keynote speaker rehearsed and re-rehearsed and, looking up from his script, found me drawn with hunger and fatigue and ordered steaks for both of us; and, through a late dinner, talked to me as if I were not young or poor or Brooklyn-accented, though he was head of a great company and soon to become Charles Percy, senator.

In Chicago, in the summer of 1960, they sent me carrying messages and cans of film through baking streets, to be caught in a jam of people as Eisenhower rode past, sitting on the back of a convertible, his smile in a translucent face like a blessing it was impossible to forget. (For I had stood five years before within the packed cathedral in Rome and, in spite of myself, shouted *"Il Pape! Il Pape!"* as he was carried past in a chair, and tears streamed down my face; crying with a worship I did not understand but swept up, ignited by what everyone else was feeling there.) And in Chicago, too, helpless against the love and happiness pouring from the man, responding willingly to the salvation he promised us.

In Chicago, in 1960, they finally let me out and handed me a pass; and I raced up an endless succession of steps which led, as in a Doré lithograph, to the pinnacle of earth, below which I could see the twisting ribbons of color; of bobbing, gold-fringed flags with the American eagle crown; of swirling spots which crossed and recrossed and went walleyed against the packed walls of the stadium, catching in their swinging arcs the clusters of technicolored balloons released above delegates' heads; landing on the floor, they popped and burst like pistol shots.

"Mr. Speaker . . ." the voice boomed out. He mounted the steps to the speaker's podium, far, far below where I sat. I saw him through the haze of smoke from a thousand cigarettes; hands raised in the V for Victory, while the band burst and the voices rose and tumultuous adulation roared like waves across the audience and sent its ripples through the screens. This is America! This. Here. We are making history! We have caught a moment of time and made it ours, living forever. An orgy of excitement reigns. We scream his name. Up on my feet I screamed too, chanting as they did, frenzied with joy, while he stood underneath the lights and raised his arms, embracing us.

Chicago, 1960: the shouting, ringing, triumphant sounds of American life. And, much later, I am to find this description of us written by a reporter on a paper in Frankfurt, Germany. America, he says, is "divided into races, castes, minorities that are not integrated, but still spanned by a common, hardly affected feeling of greatness, power and mission so strong as to appear to outsiders like Messianic chauvinism."

Chicago, 1960, and I am a disciple, a progenitor of this greatness. Burning with vision, I will carry the message throughout the land. So that others might hear and hallucinate too.

And, much later, I find this paragraph in a book called *The Ordeal of Total War,* by Gordon Wright:

"It may be that characters warped by the experience of total war will never quite return to their former shape, and that from these warped qualities may emerge the neuroses of the next generation."

Chicago, 1960: I am the next generation. The survival of my country is up to me. I am responsible. I will succeed. But I had "forgotten how to feel because it was too dangerous," though I did not know it then. I thought I felt. It was the feeling, now that I look back, of someone who is lying in some fitful sleep where symbolic distortions mask the logic of the tales we tell ourselves. And in Chicago, in 1960, I did not know that a time would come when, against my will, the machine would falter and rip the film that was threading through my mind. And sleep would end.

There is a price to be paid by those who dream.

". . . The price a white man and a white woman will pay in themselves before they can look at me as though I was simply another human being. This metamorphosis is what we are really striving for," James Baldwin says.

Metamorphosis costs. The price we pay is waking up.

". . . when one has emptied one's heart of all human feeling, you would do anything to anybody and justify it."

Chicago, 1960: anesthetized on the wastelands of Oz, what we do is to ourselves.

In the land of the junkies, who would save an addict child?

ᘓ 2

I have paid my dues to the old year. Militant confrontations end
a decade of viewing violence. It has been my sole responsibility
to see and note; and I have assumed that responsibility well. The
Seventies have arrived. They will be, I will make them, more
serene. How? I do not know. I have no plan. But I know I must
somehow.

Perhaps the answer lies with Edward Brooke, for it is serenity
I find in his finely pressed image as it unwinds through the glass.
His modulated, cultivated voice betrays no regional origin. It is
a universal, American speech he uses in propounding our legends to a gathering of children, red and black and brown, who
sit listening to the senator respectfully; as once I did when illu-
sion was the only reality I knew, and I could not know or believe
that what they told us might not be true.

The senator, believing, recites a hymn:

"A greater race than ere the world has known shall rise,
With freedom in their souls and the light of knowledge
    in their eyes.

They shall be gentle, brave and strong to spill no drop
   of blood . . ."

and, listening to him, I wonder where such people will come
from for, among men, no archangels can exist; and saviors must,
necessarily, die.

But the senator, believing in the processes of democracy, believes also there is a way to the creation of the suprahuman
being; and he tells the children why and how.

"I remember when I was a young boy I had a grandmother who
used to say to me, 'Edward, remember your place.' You may not
know what she meant at that time, but I did, and her admonition
to me was based upon her desire to protect me.

"Perhaps some of you have had your parents or your grandpar-
ents say to you, 'Remember your place at all times,' meaning
thereby that you should never get out of your place because it
might be injurious to you."

Don't anger them.

"I understood and I was most sympathetic with my grandmother, but the advice was always something that disturbed me,
because I always believed, and I ask you to believe, that your
place on this earth is any place you want to make it," the senator
says earnestly, fatherlike.

"I suggest to you that you be self-sufficient and independent.
No matter what your opportunities may be, try to walk as far as
you can by yourself. . . ."

In the forests of the frontier, no one will come to pull you out.

"I am not suggesting the easiest course here. Perhaps you've
seen a stagnant pool somewhere along the way. It's usually accompanied by a growth around it and an odor which is not very
pleasant. It is not moving. . . .

"Life was never intended to be a stagnant pool. I say to you, go
out into the stream, into the rapids. Oh, it might be dangerous
and you might get some cuts along the way . . ."

Or holes penetrating behind your brain.

79

". . . and some bruises. But it will be exhilarating and bracing . . ."

You will not breathe.

". . . and you'll be alive and you'll be moving and you'll be living and you will get great reward for having made the swim."

You'll drown.

Well, they told me that too, when I was young. In 1942 the President said: "Our earth is but a small star in the great universe. Yet of it we can make, if we choose, a planet unvexed by war, untroubled by hunger or fear, undivided by senseless distinctions of race, color or theory." He was one of the Big Three, the triumvirate of men, the Trinity. "If we choose," and of course we would. Who would resist? "If we choose," he said; all dreams were possibilities; and destiny, life itself, was what we chose to make it for ourselves.

But Brooke does not acknowledge, does not describe to his young audience what makes a rapid of a stream; nor does he tell them of the invisible, immutable natural law that seasonally disrupts the water flow; nor does he ever describe what happens to the swimmer when, overnight, frost descends and the graying winter starts. No matter how strong, no swimmer survives such temperatures.

There are no warnings. But there should be; for in the Sixties we had developed the science of cryogenics to a perfect degree; and preserved ourselves in preplanned ways.

As the Sixties began, I was working on campaign films. I viewed, I listened, I took notes. But I did not really hear as the producer said, "People vote with their glands," and then proceeded with charts and graphs to plot injection points; proceeded to mark off and isolate the organs useful to us; proceeded to cut and splice with film and sound; proceeded, and succeeded in teaching me, how to rearrange responses as Pavlov did. But what I did not understand is that, in the process, I was also performing these experiments on myself.

Nor were we alone, experimenting in an isolated way in one political laboratory. For, by the beginning of the Sixties, film was carried to election wars. Twenty years before we had sat in darkened movie theaters while our country injected us with truth. Now the theater had moved into our homes; and our entire nation was a subject audience: that will would triumph which most cunningly controlled—with picture, with music, with verbal track—the sluggish function of our glands.

Learning quickly, I could see the imagic advances of the other side. They created a young and shining prince, another god; and with their subtle probes pinpointed, heightened our desires. Here was the consummation the electorate desired.

I saw, I understood. But I was, to this particular symbol, peculiarly immune. For, long before, I had stopped mourning the poet's defeat, sensing dimly in some way that poetry was not enough. And thus, in a Washington hotel room on that first election of the new decade, drank from the paper cups being passed around and watched and worried because something was not right; something had gone wrong. And the next day, though I would not fully agree with the woman around whom we had gathered, still I listened as she spoke. She was of the generation before mine, highly skilled, amply rewarded with an important job in the campaign.

"I'm very worried," she said. "Very afraid of what's going to happen now."

Sadness was what I felt. But not danger. In the late-morning post-mortem, we were all very sad. She was the only one who was afraid. She did not, however, tell us why.

But if, at the beginning of the Sixties, my portrait of America still remained essentially unchanged, as the decade evolved itself, the glass through which I viewed the scene began to cloud; as if the present and future were of unequal temperature with the past.

The Bay of Pigs adds an element for which I have no name. Its sound, as if from some primitive lens mechanism, echoes from another time, from other days of infamy. "Always we will remember the character of the onslaught against us," the President said. I remember too, and watch with disbelief, as invasion is launched from our sacred shores. I close my eyes. It will go away. It cannot be. Someone will explain it all.

But no one does. Nor do they really tell us what is happening as a crisis of warheads occurs behind locked rooms. Demonic figures hide the truth as they slip in and out. Are they playing with my life? I have heard it scornfully called something else in other days: a policy of brinksmanship. Maligned, perhaps with cause. But now the waters bubble and regurgitate. They play this game again. With bombs. Will five survive? The crisis past, we breathe again. But I am uncomfortable, sitting here.

". . . Nobody knows what strings are being pulled and what we are being led into. . . ."

If I will die, I want a chance to save myself.

"They gave me up for four days," a new friend says, hobbling over to me on crutches as he talks. An automobile accident the year before has marked him permanently. He never smiles. Each movement is studied, is intense. There is something strange behind his eyes as if a burning conversion had occurred. I cannot connect him up to anything I have known, or seen; but there is, somewhere, a recognition, an awe of holiness in me; for he has been participant in the most secret rite of all, and made his novitiate into the mysteries of an ultimate pain. Idly we talk and I question him, for I somehow feel he regrets the century of his birth.

"I do," he says, and then surprises me. "I wish I was born in 2722."

An odd time to pick. Why?

"We're just beginning now," he says. "The seeds have just been planted. They take a long time to grow. By 2722 we will all have learned to love each other," he says.

There will be no manmade death, I think; and ask if there is ever love enough for all mankind. Will we have enough left for individual love?

He scorns my need. "You are talking about passion," he says. "Passion exhausts. But love fulfills and replenishes itself."

And love can never, therefore, die.

The man on crutches is not a friend for long. He makes a set of rules for his life and mine; forbids me entrance to the territory of himself. He will not wander freely where I would go. I refuse. I do not need safety yet. It is my life. I am willing to risk the cuts and bruises, for I know my country always survives.

And then, shortly after, I go to the Army's vaults . . . to see the ring of steel, to see myself; to cry, to become—for the first time —afraid. Still, it was all long ago. It will never happen again. It will never happen here.

A friend gives up her job and journeys south; and when she returns we do not talk, as we once did, of men and dates and clothes and work. She is impatient with me, cuts me out.

"You don't understand what's happening down there."

I don't. Nor do I understand her; or understand, either, the sudden distance that has appeared between us, ending the laughter we used to share. She has become, to me, like one of those gaunt women who have defleshed their bodies with their faith. I cannot understand why she has become this way: for once I used to admire the graceful simplicity of her dress, the aura of quiet assurance she carried with her always; and I would watch and try to learn the classic art of womanhood she practiced so successfully. But now all that is gone. She has been on a Freedom Ride, and it has destroyed the magic she once was able to exercise over all of us who knew and welcomed her into our lives. And when I question other friends they shrug their shoulders helplessly; for none of us can find the answer to aberrations such as these.

Through the decade, I continue to observe. I watch and turn the film by day; and, at night, come home to other stories on the screen. One night there is a play on a favorite series; and a line jumps out at me. I rush to make a note of it, though I do not really know why.

"When a child plays with a doll, she knows that the doll is not alive. But she wants so much to believe the doll is alive, that for a moment it is—in the child's mind.

"In this fashion, if I were to tell you I am the Queen of Spain, for a little while I would be, and live in enchantment," the character says.

The Queen of Spain, for whom enchantment comes by total

belief. But is there another side to this? For all fairy tales have in them wickedness, violence and villainy. And if I am the Queen of Spain, and my enchanted garden suddenly becomes an oozing swamp, then what is true is that the oozing swamp would be real as well.

And then over what would I preside? A subject, in what danger would I be?

The sound of drums rolls over the entire world: the waves of each deep beat meeting, crossing and passing each other over the city, the country, other lands which—all—stand paralyzed and dull in the fall sunshine. There is no other sound but this slow tattoo, commemorating national patricide.

Far below me, in the street, where traffic normally honks and bustles its way among the lights and too-narrow boulevards, below me there is only silence. Horns do not trumpet anger; shouts do not betray an undirected rage. There is no sound. Only the drums, as we sit and mourn before a box.

I turn it off. I do not wish to hear, guilty at my inability to face what it is I see. But turning off the set is of no use; for I can hear the sounds coming through the window open to the fresh fall air. Why is there sun on such a day? I have had enough. Like a small cotton ball, I can absorb no more; for what has suddenly soaked me through has exceeded my own weight. I am drowning. Why? I cannot mourn a man I never loved. Her dignity puzzles me. I wonder why she does not cry, for I am beginning to. I cannot mourn a man I never loved. Whose death is it, then, I feel? Who is it who has killed? Who is it who has died? Is there murder here? And if he was not safe, could die, then what of me? Who is it who will save my life when, in the middle of the stream, someone could pull the consecrated prow-figure down?

My reputation grows. Calls come to me from all over the world. I am becoming, oddly, that typical American, the small-business entrepreneur. It is odd, for I have never thought of myself this way: not of books and balance sheets but of books and great words; of images strung together on paper and celluloid; of words and sound and music and camera paintings of shadow and shafts

84

of sun. But, somehow, there are obstacles to all of that. I am not quite certain why. Is there something wrong with me? It is a question I cannot decide, for other questions have intruded themselves into the simple concept of career. A woman producer for whom I work hitches up her skirt and swings her legs up on the surface of a cluttered desk. She swears upon the phone, prodding recalcitrant laboratories who have been slow in processing our film; she gives up smoking cigarettes and takes to smoking small cigars which dangle from her uncosmeticized lips as she haggles with cameramen and hassles the grips whose precious union time eats up the budgetary dollars she must disburse and oversee. Once we were friends too. "We're making movies," she had said to me one day, giggling; as if, for her, a dream-game had come true. But I had watched her body language translate itself into something else and knew I was not born to rule: not this way; and had retreated, then, into my gentle business in which I ran only me; and filled orders for film and accepted fees and quietly probed producers' imaginings to find out what they saw and then use what they saw in the retinal selection I made for them.

I am a very special specialist. My phone rings often, jobs pile upon jobs: a thousand, fifteen hundred, two thousand dollars a week. I handle three and four assignments at once; working late into the night; working weekends; proud of my growing bank account. But absorbed, too, by what I see, and caring for each individual film's excellence.

I am swimming through sixty years of film: immersed, entangled, and with a growing sense of history; participant in the process again as, one year, I listen to the candidate who says, "Extremism in the defense of liberty is no vice . . . and moderation in the pursuit of justice is no virtue." Though he is of my party, I am not impressed by the man. Still, I am puzzled by the outcry following his words; for what has he said that is different from what we have always believed? Justice must be pursued by an immoderate course if justice can be obtained no differently. We must be relentless, always on guard against infringement on what is just, on what is right; and, if liberty is endangered, must we not—have we not always—taken extreme measures in its defense? I cannot understand the liberals' arguments that blaze in the Film Center coffee shop; for they do blaze immoderately. I am puzzled, for there is no simple disagreement here but the violence of an emotion I cannot condone.

I do understand, I think, but do not trust the other candidate, who says, "I will not send American boys to fight an Asian war." The dangers are of a decade before; and to avert the catastrophic loss, our Everyman President brandished the constitutional weapon of civilian rule. Still, I am puzzled also by the principle here, for I still see the man standing on the steps of the primitive plane brandishing a piece of paper in the airfield wind and pronouncing it a treaty for "peace in our time." Geography changes. History stands still. And, though I cannot help but approve of actions of succeeding years, there is something in the drawling, monotonic voice which I find threatening; as if there is something subtly devious, an aberration hidden from my sight; a darkness of vision I cannot really grasp. "People vote with their glands." I shrug it off, thinking that perhaps I think that way as well, for who can accurately schematize a Russian soul? And the Presidency is an office which, for the lone citizen who is me, is not easily challenged. The idea of office is like a rule learned elementally. It is a commandment handed down by a higher power; an abstract, disembodied force that is supernatural and therefore beyond contesting by human thought.

One afternoon, wandering distractedly from my small apartment, I stand in Riverside Park and look north and west across the Hudson River, which separates two states. It is not really riverlike, I think; smiling at the long-ago descriptions of the boys poling their way on a raft down what had become—in my mind —what a river really was. The Hudson was not a river, simply a kind of channel, a trench, from whose sides there rose—across the way—the steep cliffs of the Palisades; which, on certain shrouded nights, became more than croppings of rock; became, on those nights, like canyons: mysterious, hidden, immortal, beautiful.

Suppose I were the Palisades: my mind wanders, reshaping

itself. I am immobile, immovable—except of course for TNT—
and standing rock-proud, people look across at me and say, "Isn't
that beautiful? Look at the simple, unembellished wonder of that
cliff: power in its natural form." But what do I give, standing
there? I cannot move. I am aware that I am admired, but what
meaning is there in that? I stand there, watching them as they
swim up and down the highway in their frail vehicles, as the tiny
figures wander over the river path and stand and look at the
water below and gaze, unseeing, at the vast simplicity of me; as
the dayliners and tugs and little power craft throb and toot and
buck underneath my overhang. What do I give? I am rooted in the
earth, deep under the surface, and only violence can blast me
loose. I cannot move. I am a natural obstacle; and the nature of
me is also the obstacle of me.

Perhaps, I think, now splitting myself into an antagonist,
someone would say, "Wouldn't it be nice if we could transport it
here, to be a living, functional part of our lives."

The antagonist itself splits; and then says, "Well, it's a nice
idea. But you can't transport a palisade."

And the first antagonist says, "No. I guess not. I guess not without destroying what a palisade is."

I guess you're right. No one can bring me across that river. And
I cannot bring myself. And so I stand aloof, rising majestically,
a God-given wonder, unlike most other things in the world. If I
am unique, strong and distinct, I am—also—all alone.

And my patient big-sister friend Eleanor says, "What a habit
you have of cutting everyone off!"

I sense her hurt, but do not explain; for how can I explain to
anyone where it is I go when I cut them off; for I do not really
know myself.

Nor can I explain to her, or anyone, what happens to me on the
day *The Pawnbroker*, Nazerman, comes into my life; and the
subliminal cuts of his concentrated recall are like signal shades
drawn swiftly up and down in me too. For, somewhere, someone
has found a way to project the processes of my mind; and in the
movie theater I journey with Nazerman—I am Nazerman—back
and forth in time; until for me, too, the inner evisceration can no

longer be borne behind the tensed musculature and an inhuman issuance of sound occurs; and, turning, the wounded animal is forced to feed itself on its own kind in order to remain alive. But I am not, am not, afraid. My apartment is in an area of high crime; yet I can walk late at night down its streets with no apprehension ticking inside, no loss of comfort, no fear. I can—and do —ski the narrowest, iciest slopes; and the dangers of such places are, for me, at some distance so far, far away that they are beyond my ability to grasp the shape and outline of them.

I am not afraid. Of what is there to be afraid? I am doing . . . nothing. I do not contest. Yet, after being Nazerman, I feel a gathering; as if soon, soon . . . it is coming. The thunder, far off, is still perceptible. Yet I cannot wrench the sounds of it from inside my brain; I cannot find the notes and set them down within a scale; I cannot link them together to create some kind of picture that will tell someone something. For I do not know what something is: only that it is. There is something about something that I wish to say. But what? And why is it that no one can hear that I am hearing something? Why is it that there is, nowhere, any human being with an organic stapes of such flexibility that—more than human—it can make music of, can tell me, transcribe, give form to what I hear; that, hearing, can turn to me and say, "Yes, yes, I am listening; and it is very beautiful. Did that great song come from you?" Are you all deaf, and blind, that you can't see inside me and know that there is a melodic rainbow there?

But they can't see, of course they can't see, and I wonder why I expect them to. "Someday the prince will come. . . ." Someday, somehow, somewhere; and the music of that song fills me and I dream of my promised land and wait, imprisoned, in my enchanted tree. It will all be over soon, I think: lightning will strike; I will be freed, like Veronica Lake. But when that happens, I ask myself, will "I" be freed a living thing, or will there only be a shade of the "I" left; a ghost, for I will be long since dead?

One day, with a friend, I go to hear a new savior speak. In the converted theater on the Lower East Side, we watch as colors strobe across the stage and strange strings raga ever more rhythmically. My friend and I watch and then turn to each other and smile, incredulously; incredulous that we should have spent money to see a medicine show. Yet we grow chilled as we sit there, for the audience listens enraptured as the white-pajamaed prophet speaks; and they respond in frenzy to the incantations of his chemically abrogated brain. "Tune in, turn on, drop out," he preaches at them. And, as we wander from the theater, we begin to wonder if freedom of speech allows an audience to stand on the sidewalk far below yelling "Jump! Jump!" to the damaged, agonized creature who wishes to leap down and splatter himself at their feet. What weapons do we have when someone is free to chant "drop out," "turn on"? And I read Daniel Freedman's description: ". . . the shifts and strains inherent in the experience of the potentially most unstable group of any society—the adolescent and the young adult." In America, have we ceased to protect our young? Has freedom extended itself so far that freedom itself has become a danger to our species which our young will not survive?

Turn on, drop out. It is easy to rebel, not to accept. It is much more difficult, more agonizing to realize, I think, what must be: to accept what must be because I have learned that I cannot change what is. Life consists of a series of going-ons: I write a note to myself.

Treading water, one day I see something I cannot believe. The filmmakers have begun to concentrate on epics of the latest war. And researching for them, in my glass I see an immobile man sitting cross-legged upon the ground. There is a sudden flame, like that of the flash paper sold at magic stores; and then the man topples over as if he were an incinerated flower pod. The Buddhist monk set himself on fire. I cannot believe that was once a living thing I saw. Yet, in my screen, as I follow the war, I see others who do not deliberately choose such deaths. Or, perhaps, such deaths were for them, too, only like imaginings seen so far away they had no shape and outline which could be understood. But I understand. In Vietnam, I watch, horrified, as the color camera closes in to record two men scraping the charred pilot from the seat of his plane; and the film remains in my archive like a permanent record which will never disintegrate.

In a newspaper column, I read as Max Lerner describes "modern man in another phase, converting political movements into political religions and filling even a mild religion like Buddhism with the fire of political creed." I understand, for I have been brought up with the articles of faith, and my hymns are called: "America the beautiful . . ."

Max Lerner also writes of Nietzsche, who "thought the Christian doctrine of humility and pacifism in the face of evil was an impossible doctrine, and that the repression of the passions went against the grain of man's nature which lay in struggle and conflict."

He also writes: "There are three facets of man's nature: he is man the killer; he is man the brother, the social being; he is man alone, solitary, hungry to be linked with something outside himself. . . . We have not tamed the killer in man. We have at times over-politicized the social man, making of him too often a political True Believer. We have not yet found an adequate dialogue for the man who stands alone whether with God or with his fellow man."

In a tower in Texas, a man stands alone and, with rifle and bullet clips, holds off the police for many hours as, one by one, he shoots the living citizens down. Charles Whitman invades and then leaves a terrible memorial with me; for though I do not understand why, when I hear of him there is a sudden surge of his rage which also flows through me. There is no world, I think, in which I will be absolutely safe, as I watch and hear the film which begins to speed up and amplify itself as I sit turning it day after day; as riots begin, are faced and end; as students on campuses protest and chant and try to tear down our flag, substituting it with that of the enemy; and then are allowed to go unpunished, are allowed to go free, when I would not have been. Where is such privilege in this land where all have equal rights and penalties are equally prescribed? What are they tearing away with their reedy voices crawling across the screen countryside, leaving in their wake an uncollected excrement? Why do we listen to such voices, our storm trooper young who will, one day, form themselves under some twisted cross behind a mad hysteric and burn down the walls of government? Does no one see? Does no one understand? I am not safe. No one is listening, Charles Whitman, up in the tower; and one day someone will come with nailed boots and kick down the door; and you will find that you are defending nothing at all with your immortal beliefs. They will take you away and you will find life has been a big con game and somebody cheated you. Who is it who promised anyway?

Endangered, Charles Whitman fights back: in the face of evil, his struggle and conflict takes terrible form. Behind his primeval fury is an agony for which murder is the only way out. To murder and then to kill yourself. So that it will all end, for the pain is killing you. Get it over with. You have no strength left anymore, except for this one last bursting of the will.

But I am not mad, or weak. I cannot kill. "Kill or be killed," the general said. But the gnarled and twisted stick was dropped on that Brooklyn playfield a long time ago; and the field, now, is covered over, tarred. It is a parking lot and at the other end there stands a strange bank shaped like the rounded tower of the fort in New York Bay. The neighborhood has changed. My mother moves to Forest Hills. Childhood is gone; nature's course is inevitable. Truth has changed; and the truths of adulthood are different from those of a child. It is difficult to accept. It makes me sad. But sadness is like some kind of background score, a strain of orchestra dimly heard. It is a calming melody and inside I think, "Hush, they're gone," and I am grateful. "Learn to be alone," I tell myself. Nobody else hears the hymn.

And, alone, I take the hymn with me out to the wildly growing island; and, alone, celebrate the rite of midsummer's eve; wrapped in a blanket, huddled on the silvered beach while the grunions flash within the sea.

The moon glows hot in the sky. It makes a peculiar kind of daylight in the inky darkness. And it reflects white. So that white shines like an ornament itself. The beach is white, and in the sea little silvery points flash and fade and flash again in another place, running up and down the ripples of the waves like sequins which hit the light for only an instant and then subside behind the fold of black velvet wave.

Nearby, across the sand spit which is what the island really is, there is music flowing, weaving through the narrow concrete paths, between the top-heavy shack-houses we rent. And on the beach, shadows reflect on the sand from upper decks as the shadows slowly revolve in the moonlight, in the flowing music.

But the beach itself is still, with only the waves whispering; only the silvery waves to witness the midsummer rite . . . and I am hidden away, wrapped in my blanket, inside a hollow of grassy dune, while I listen to the laughter that descends from the upper decks and comes fluting along the beach where now silhouetted figures call tag and race each other at water's edge. I watch. They run to the sea and dip their toes into the wash of silver and tussle and fall on the white hot sand. They come together briefly, quickly, pulling away. And then run, laughing, back to the walk, back to the music, to cling again and make love under the open sky.

On midsummer's eve, under the moon, when the grunions are running into the sea, I do not question what or why or even how. I do not speak. It is not allowed. And, later, quietly rise and float to where the music is and stand in a corner of the room and know that I cannot speak; and know, too, that there is no one to hear or see. For now that I am grown, I have grown invisible. I have lost the spirit that has nourished me. And I will never be visible ever again.

And, invisible, far away where they cannot see me, I also watch, shivering, for the moon has gone down, as the soldiers crouch behind shining red machines and fire their rifles at figures silhouetted on rooftops who are firing back; and I cringe as tanks roll down cobbled streets. For the tanks bear white five-pointed stars on their sides, and it has been more than twenty years since I saw the flat-bedded tanks cross our summer town heading for the enemy. And, wrapped, I sit stunned as young faces peep from under khaki helmets, watching warily behind machine gun nests emplanted on the marbled balconies of our nation's capitol.

Here? Here! It cannot be. I am confused. I often cry. But no one sees. For I have learned the scent of fear is, itself, dangerous. And my face echoes nothing day after day, as I play poker with the world.

King dies. And, with sympathy for the bereavement of others, I turn the reels slowly through the machine and catch a glimpse, remembering later on, of the thin and silent face of Bobby Kennedy, upon whom a fragment of light falls from the stained-glass window of the church.

And then, one day, it is Bobby Kennedy who becomes a subject for a film; and I follow him on the last campaign, to hear him speak of King. "With his death the drums are louder," Bobby says. "We do not know yet whether we will be summoned to battle or to a reconciliation. . . ."

He crisscrosses the country, journeying further into it than I have been. Signs meet him at whistle stops. A girl waves one: "I Love Ruthless Men," it says. What does it take to govern? I ask myself.

And then I find him standing in a circle of light created for him by some cameraman, subconsciously perhaps. His shirt is open, sleeves rolled up, tie loosened beneath a bony throat. As he speaks, I am mesmerized, as are the others watching there. This is no campaign document, but the uncut material straight from the network reel. He believes, he believes. I feel. He tells us, believing, "One individual can make the difference," he says. "You, too, can make a difference," he says.

Bobby is shot. I see that too. I am there, in the frenzied crowd where young girls with long blond hair who wear red-white-and-blue paper hats sit weeping on the stage where he has just stood. Go west. And I wait beside the white ambulance in the somber concrete hospital yard as people enter and leave the swinging entrance door and no one speaks and we wait, hushed, for some word. He cannot die.

And then the train: with Sandburg images it winds through the

93

June countryside, all green; passing the little houses from which there hang flags at half mast; past railroad stations lined four deep with a tribute of human bodies, many of whom cry and rub their eyes; past crossings where cars are halted, waiting, while standing outside their occupants salute and some, heads bowed, put hands over hearts in a simple gesture of sadness, fealty and pain.

To make a difference it is necessary to know what to change; in order to change it is necessary first to be. But "to be" does not compute. How do you do that? And if you are still wondering how "to be" you are still far away from the answer.

What am I? What are we? What kind of creatures carry dark Bobby deaths inside? It is a terrible risk to look into a screen and see Bobby lying on a kitchen floor: to say that I did that: my nation did that. I am my nation. "Kill or be killed." The killers kill themselves: I murder others and myself. We are doing anything to anybody. How do I justify what we have done?

Weeping, mourning, I turn away from what I cannot bear to see. But they do not leave me alone, these people who live inside my head. In the bar of the sandspit to which I mechanically return year after year, I watch the streets of Chicago, where joyfully I once stood in the beginning of that decade when I became part of all this; and I watch as the multicolored helmets swirl back and forth, like on the marble gameboards of our youth: skulls like "Go" buttons advancing, retreating, spurting blood: and I see other figures running across a square, surrounded, cut off by buildings and machines as gurgled sounds issue from the track: and the nightmare has crossed the ocean at last: the stench of decay mixes with the smell of beer and suntan oil, and billiard balls click in the background above the pistol shots; and ocean and sand mingle with the gas. I watch it all and drink and stand about and shrink against the walls, for I know I am invisible anyway: and they have become invisible to me. I cannot touch them, see or hear them anymore. And one day a friend finds me, hidden out on the back porch of our little pink frame house, and she says, "Do you want something to eat? I'll fix it for you."

94

You'll fix it for me. Why would you do that?

"It's your birthday," she says.

I had forgotten the day commemorating the day I was born, the day the *Morro Castle* burned. I saw that too. I had forgotten that I once could feel; and then I learned; and learning sent me back to sleep where, within the subconscious world, I could curl up into a ball, a shape of order, where order reigned. For I had learned that freedom was pain; it threatened; I might not su.-vive.

We invoke our own martyrdoms; and, like martyrs, passionately burn ourselves to death for a cause.

"Passion exhausts. Love fulfills," the crippled man had said many years ago. But exhaustion comes in a multiplicity of strains; and some exhaustion is the final lingering, the final giving up; while other exhaustion is but the quiet process of sitting silent, remembering; allowing ourselves to mourn what once was and will never be again.

"There is no greater pain than to recall a happy time in wretchedness."

The happy time was childhood, filled with innocence. But we are children no more; and now have the components of a mature, developed passion with which to contend. Passion exhausts: and returning feeling causes the inner streams of consciousness to meet in currents that conflict. A sucking whirlpool tries to pull us down. We fight, are flung upon the rocks and micaed promontories.

Among the studies on the effects of war, I find these words in a book called *Problems of Social Policy,* by R. M. Titmuss:

"Perhaps more harm was wrought to the minds and to the hearts of men, women and children than to their bodies. The disturbances to family life, the separation . . . of society from the pursuits of peace—perhaps all of these indignities of war have left wounds which will take time to heal and infinite patience to understand."

War in childhood, war again at a time when wounds are hardly healed. Cut and bruised, there is great pain.

But, says Margaret Mead, in a piece of film I discover one day and view out of usual compulsiveness; but, says Margaret Mead, in Europe there is still "a belief that some measure of pain is man's lot in the world," and in this country too, "the Catholic Church has stood for facing grief. Whereas on the whole, the Protestant and secularized community has abandoned grief, or attempted to abandon the recognition of grief for a very long time. . . .

"The newer American ethic is that you shouldn't have to meet ups and downs that aren't necessary. . . . We do not believe as a people in unnecessary suffering."

But in the serenity of the Seventies I am now entering, I have found Rap Brown, who has reversed the ethic and thrown it in my face:

"People recognize, and the poor people recognized first, what it takes to get freedom in America."

What it takes is facing pain: allowing agony: to be visible.

". . . you will be fighting and you will be moving," Edward Brooke has also said.

Is it, has it always been a dream I've seen? Or could the dream come true? And what is the price we must pay for freedom, for liberty: for life itself?

"You, too, can make a difference."

Bobby is dead. The cost is great: the risk perhaps too much to demand of myself. Perhaps it is better to be still, to give up. The Seventies are here. But it is not quiet yet. There must be some way out of pain: to protect and, at once, to preserve myself.

How do I get what I want?

Who will teach me what I need to know?

The Austrian, I decide. He seems to have found the way; and so, observing, I study him: to see him, week after week, return to the same place and to the same people; to see him comfortable and laughing in his place; to see him greet each new skiing day joyfully as he comes tumbling down the stairs, welcomed and welcoming; with bursting energy warming us.

And, one morning, he comes upon me as I sit morosely in front of the window in the lodge at Pico Peak, fiddling with my boots;

trying to wake myself up. Since childhood, I have hated all mornings: daybreak is my enemy.

I am hunched over, struggling with the laces of my inner boot. I look up to see him smiling down at me.

"Come, we take a little social run," he says.

I wave him away. "Not now, thanks." It will take me too long to put on my boots; I do not ski well in the morning anyway; above all, I will be too self-conscious to ski with him, for he has been racing mountains since he was a little boy. I am grumpy. I wave him away.

He turns. "Later perhaps," and walks away.

He is refused. But later, when I do seek him out, he says, "I wish to be alone now," and crossing the practice slope, slashes his way through the slalom poles and then is gone; to some place on the mountainside where I cannot follow him; and, in the evening, when I am surfeited with *Gemütlichkeit;* when I am growing claustrophobic among the strangers; when it becomes difficult to contend with the slapping, stamping, climbing songs of mixed male voices and the sweet registers of the women: then, when later in the evening I need to get away, to become myself again, to walk down the road to the stand of pines over which the moon we have just reached glows white, and the frozen lake flashes with the sparkled flakes of snow; when, later in the evening, I ask him to take a walk with me, I am refused. And he turns the cashmere-sweatered back, rests his elbows on the bar, and continues to fill his glass; to drink, to fill it again. He is quiet. He speaks to no one. He does not laugh.

And, morosely, I go shuffling out; to stand under the trees, remembering the songs I have just heard, and see the white expanse of frozen lake, its borders outlined by the dark, jagged pines that look black in the night. I look back at where I have been. The lights of the house glitter in the frosting air. There is an even line of them on the first floor; but on the two floors above, they scatter fitfully, like an electric sign with some of the bulbs gone dead.

Shivering, I look forward again and see, coming across the ice, dim figures slipping soundless across the frozen snow. They have not seen me yet. But soon, soon. They track with skill. Is the Austrian among them? I do not know. But I must not wait for their approach. I know somehow they're dangerous. I must get away from here. And so, hurrying, wading through the drifted banks, I short-cut to the road and stand, hidden for a moment behind a tree, as the scraping snowplow shoots its beam and scrapes metal with a flash of sparks, like some prehistoric machine that breathes past me, cycloptic, unseeing. And when its eye passes me, I hurry back to the house, where the Austrian is still drinking at the bar. His eyes grow narrow. He does not see me as I cross the room. But I will not call his attention to me again; and, alone, I mount the shadowed stairs and go to bed. I am very tired, but I cannot sleep. And for many hours toss out there in space, carrying on a burning dialogue with myself.

I am refused.

What does it take to get freedom in America? Impassioned, I am exhausted by my belief. But I still remember the legendary place about which I have been told. Where will I get the strength to find serenity and fulfillment too? Must I choose the dream . . . and pain?

I am refused. If I turn away, give up, will the pain go away too?

What is the price of serenity? What difference does it make what I decide? The universe has an order all its own. Against its decisions, I am helpless to change.

⤙ 3

Helpless, helpless, I am trapped: pulled by my nation into a quicksand pit. I am abandoned, tired . . . and alone. I no longer have the strength to answer Baldwin's call to arms.

". . . It is a vitality . . . which allows you to believe, and to act on the belief, that it is your country. And your responsibility to your country is to free it."

My country has imprisoned me. Those who have been forgotten, whose solitary voice is too gentle a whisper to be heard, cannot even free themselves.

"In order to free it you have to change it. And you can't do that."

I can't. I know. And so I sit staring into the stagnant pool from which I have half crawled, the evolutionary process stopped. I am a doomed mutant, after all: one of nature's mistakes. I will not survive.

But now the underground poisons pressure their way to the top. Gaseous bubbles emitted from black wells insist on parting webs of slime. It is not safe to remain. The odor asphyxiates. I cannot breathe. I must get away from here. Where shall I go? And what will happen to me there?

In one of the newspapers of the time I read this excerpted

quote. It is from a book called *On Becoming a Person,* by Carl Rogers:

"In our daily lives there are a thousand and one reasons for not letting ourselves experience our attitudes fully, reasons from the past and from the present, reasons that reside within the social situation. It seems dangerous, too potentially damaging. . . . But in the safety and freedom of the therapeutic relationship, they can be experienced fully, clear to the limit of what they are . . . so that for the moment the person *is* his fear, or he *is* his anger, or he *is* his tenderness. . . ."

I am . . . nothing yet. I have not emerged to become: in process: processing myself: unaware of where I am. I live my life within the sprocket rollers and reflecting glass of a small hand viewing machine: still held within the frames of black.

In this way, early one morning, I meet Sidney Poitier, and find a gaggle of newsmen questioning him. The film is dated 1967. It is the summer of riot. Behind the cameras, the reporters thrust questions about Hollywood first.

And then:

"What do you feel Rap Brown's purpose is now?" they ask.

Poitier looks beyond the lights. "I figured that question would come," he says sardonically. "I'm not familiar with all of Mr. Brown's methods, except Mr. Brown suggests violence. Well, I am, always, by definition, in opposition to violence, particularly violence for violence's sake."

The reporters do not let up. "Do you think the urban riots have affected [your position] though?"

"I would say that the urban riots have had effects in every corner of the country and in every arena of life." Poitier's voice gathers itself in his throat.

Still, the reporters persist. "Now what do you feel he's creating?" Being black, Poitier is naturally an expert on Rap Brown.

Poitier leans forward, clenches his hands in front of him and asks a question of his own. He speaks clearly, slowly, each word enunciated with a precision he carefully controls. The soft Caribbean sounds flicker warnings of a storm.

"Why is it you guys are such hounds for bad news?"

Why is it that producers jump on their Movieola seats when I bring them bloody images to view?

Poitier continues.

"You know, it seems to me that at this moment, this day, you could ask me many questions about many positive and wonderful things that are happening in this country. . . ."

Mesmerized themselves, television's newsmen cannot themselves see what is good and wonderful here. And when I watch their film, neither can I. Our images are both product and raw material fed by juices of our glands.

"I'm a relatively intelligent man. There are many aspects to my personality that you can explore, I think, very constructively. . . . But we gather here to pay court to sensationalism. We gather here to pay court to negativism. . . . You sit here and ask me one-dimensional questions that fall continually within the Negroness of my life. You ask me questions that pertain to the narrow scope of the summer riots.

"I'm artist. Man. American. Contemporary. I'm an awful lot of things. So I wish you would pay me the respect due and not simply ask me about those things!"

Behind the cameras, applause rings out. Absently I make a note of it, for I am thinking deeply of what he has just said. Man. Contemporary. American. Artist. Descriptives of great simplicity: in combination most complex. Staring at the face magnified by the mirrors of the machine, I see a man unafraid of himself and therefore able to contend with the flecks of dirt within us all; and, denying our denial, using a very human anger to lance our crusted sores.

I am puzzled. They applauded him! But Rap Brown was angry too. Why did I want to kill? What is the difference here? I, too, am conscious of angers deep inside. No cameras make a record of my rage. I follow the disciplined rules of polite society, and sweetly have answered questions such as those asked me at a Massachusetts resort.

"I'm sorry, but I haven't the faintest idea how to make a blintz."

Nor have I done more than sadly store my typewriter away

when an editor writes back, "You are, indeed, a woman's writer."

Controlled, I turn from grief and do not mourn. Life consists simply of a series of going-ons.

One day, toward the end of the decade, a man who is to be the last of my own "little adventures" has found me standing, crying, in the middle of a slope: frustrated and angry at myself because I am unable to swoop down this most expert, narrow, steeply banked trail as I wish to, as I know I somehow could if I somehow could discover the secret that is eluding me.

"Well, so you can't ski this," he says. "No reason why you really should. It's a bad mother." He smiles and looks up at me. "But you can ski all the others. So you can't ski this. Give up. You just can't ski it." He shrugs his shoulders, his poles swinging loose above his skis.

"I can't give up," I tell him. "I can't give up."

He is standing just below me on the slope which is named Paradise . . . tauntingly. He looks up. Behind his goggles with the green-tinted mask, I can see his eyes grow dark. "What's wrong with giving up if you can't do something?" he asks. "What's wrong with giving up?"

I do not know. Perhaps he's right. And as he slowly skis in front of me, bringing me down—for my legs do not work—I wonder, contending with the sadness I feel knowing that in my lifetime I will never ski here again.

But later in the evening, much later, after everyone has gone to bed, I hear a drumbeat softly throbbing at my door. He must be playing, I think, for my last adventure is a musician who had given up a scholarship to Juilliard for the security of a construction-union membership. I creep out of bed and, barefooted, walk carefully half down the stairs of the old house a group of us have rented for the wintertime.

The fire is still flickering in the old, unlovely fireplace. The drumbeats are louder. Curling up on the threadbare stairs, I peek down into the living room, through the Jacobean balustrade.

He is seated, cross-legged, on the floor, turned sideways to the stair. Between his legs there are two small bongo drums, on which he is beating softly; his fingers moving singly, sometimes,

sometimes in pairs, each hand separated from but attached with some invisible wire to the other. His face is in profile, and I can watch it as it changes, looks inside. His eyes are half closed, head tilted to one side. He is listening to something, something I cannot hear, something no one else can hear but him. The flames flicker their shadows across his face, masking and unmasking his eyes. But he sees nothing: not the room nor the fire nor even this moment of life. And I begin to hear something I have never heard in him before, some sound coming from deep within: a secret he has with himself; lonely, anguished, very sad.

I watch him for a long, long time. On two simple, primitive drums he is making a statement which is a testament of resignation, defeat . . . despair.

I will not tell him that I heard. And, after a little while, I turn away and go back to bed, closing the door on the music still welling, like a secret ache, from the man before the fire.

"What's wrong with giving up?" he asked.

What's wrong with giving up, I think, is the way giving up multiplies itself.

And when, later, in late spring, I repeatedly encourage him to return to music, to take a chance, what my last adventure gives up is me.

"It makes no difference what you are," I tell Poitier, with whom I have a dialogue for the rest of the day; whose attentive face remains silently in the back of my mind. "It makes no difference what you are." They have labeled you. You will carry them forever with you through your life. The world appraises me in several ways, but the words they use are of one dimension alone. I am only what they see I am: a paper figure with little tabs on which a simple costume is hung. I cannot stand on my own. Their hands must hold me up. Without them I will fall to the ground and some boot will pass and, unseeing, step where it is I am; leaving its muddied footprint on my self; pushing me into the earth where I will decay, return to dust.

If no one holds me, I will not be there. I must not anger them. I must not fight. Still, I cannot help thinking that there is some secret to me, some dimension invisible as yet to my eyes. I used to think I was a lot of things; I used to think ... when I was a little girl. Where is the respect due what I am?

Fulfilling his role, Poitier insists I must search alone for such answers. He will not speak.

I turn for answers to the two men for whom I work. "How long?" I ask; for, when I joined them, they waved promises at me; and painted pictures of feature films and television specials to write and direct.

"How long?" I question them. I have been working for them for a year. We had timed a production for now. I send them long memos filled with ideas.

"How long?" I need to do something with myself.

Their responses are recession-filled; laden with the politics of television sales. "We are fighting to keep this company up," they say.

"Right now the money is in schools," they say.

"A little while longer," they say.

"It all takes time," they say.

Time. Time. It is slipping away, my world is going over the edge. It went over once before, years before, when I was hired to make a film. It was a complicated piece of work they called for: low budget, but it still must be in color, have three screens, and sound must come from a stereophonic track.

I had been fevered with the idea; bursting with challenge; for the film they had asked me to make was a visual descriptive of what the psychology of technology had done to man.

And as I explored the film I viewed, as I pieced together idea after idea, I had seen a confusion of realities which met in Nietzschean conflict as our minds gave birth to all of our primitive, dark dreams.

I was immersed, excited; worked late into the night, punching up on the center screen the result and then splitting the image into its component parts. Sounds filtered into my sleep. Exhausted, still I worked, hypnotized by the violence I saw in every frame of film; working with it, matching it, using it. I would not only show an audience our world, I would make them feel it; and submitted to the executive my charts and graphs, like the ones

104

he had shown me how to make when I worked for him on the campaign films. I will make them feel: and plotted pressure points, where the shock injections should be; dividing the world neatly into minute-second intervals.

Scanning the graphs, the producer approves. And then one day comes in to see a rough-cut of the film, where I have alternated scenes: men with gun-smoke rifles in the Hollywood West, cut to frightened faces crouching in the underbrush of the Vietnamese jungle; the bad guy bites the dust; and from the greening battle-field there blasts a scream of pain, "My leg, my leg, my God, my leg!" The leg is gone. Watching, the executive turns white and turns away. "Too strong," he says. "You can't do that to people," he says. "They won't sit still for this," he says; and recuts my film with a jingling commercial effect: buy U.S.A. The witch is dead.

Ding-dong. The witch is dead.

And writes me a letter on "questions of taste."

Be damned! I turn away, and bury myself in research again; for it is all I have to hold on to, all I have with which to haul myself back over the edge, where I stand, frozen and unmoving, while within me the levels of being rumble and clash, trying to adjust themselves; but always, ever afterward, never again quite smooth. Marked, by a barely discernible slivered line, where the break had occurred.

"It all takes time," they say. I must lean on them, for I am an innocent in the business world. What do I know? I like them both: one a caustic yet comforting man; the other, exactly my own age, full of sunshine and good will. He and I share the same dream and the same sense of responsibility to the quality of American life. But one day, standing in the doorway of my office, he says, "It's no use fighting them now. I've been thinking about what I want to do too. I agree with you. But the first thing is to make a lot of money. You know, as much money as you'll ever need. You do it their way first. Then, maybe you have a chance."

He is a talented man; both of them are more cinematically gifted than any of the producers for whom I have worked since I began more than ten years before. I must lean on their gifts, for I have chosen this road. They have promised me peace—some-

105

day. There is comfort and security and money here. For the first time in many years I do not need to maintain huge savings accounts against an unexpected drop in calls. I do not need to worry if I will survive. They protect me. Our contract is an insurance policy; and I can stay here, week after week, in my little office, and close the door or open it as I choose, and set out my books, and have room for my files, and order my desk as I like. And remain here for the rest of my life.

The winter sun glares brightly into my office, to which I return after each meeting with black; to type up my notes, to write my memos, to make long entries in my own book of ideas. The folders of experience grow. I do pre-cuts now from my own research, melding music, image and track; juggling triple assignments constantly. Something grows: episodes begin stringing themselves together deep within my consciousness, like spurting lines on a moving cardiogram. Rap Brown and Poitier bother me. Cleaver and Gregory and Carmichael—and Baldwin, most of all —flash intercuts in rising tempo even on my waking mind. I am hearing voices, and the voices, synergized by my own history, have psychedelic effect. Watching the black faces, I am hallucinating. Life has become one never-interrupted dream. But what is it I see? I do not know. Restless, I cannot remain. Restless, I need to get away.

"I'm going to Europe for a couple of weeks." The two men nod and, before I leave, hand me a generous vacation check. I am surprised. I have not expected to be paid. I have had more than a month off already this year. Still, it is nice to have. I will buy something with it. I will buy a good time.

I have not been to Austria for fifteen years; not since I met the Irish poet briefly there, and then wandered through a few cities of that small country on my own. It has been a long time, but I remember it very well. I was an American tourist then on a still-deprived continent. My cigarettes were coin and my language universally recognized. And now I had brought my American gold again, but this time to ski, and set myself down among the medieval streets of Kitzbühel, confident of my regency. Whom will I meet? What little adventure will I have? How much of the ring of mountains encircling this primitive world will I be able to ski and conquer before I leave?

On the first morning, ignoring the jet lag that makes my body feel like a mistooled jigsaw puzzle part, I rush to join a Saturday ski school class. They are not the group I will ski with through the first week, for the week does not begin until Monday at nine o'clock. But I must have a guide for this day. These mountains, I understand, are vast and complicated; not easily marked and well defined as our Vermont mountains are. It is easy to get lost. It is best to ski with someone who knows them well.

My instructor is a young, tall, dark-haired man who speaks three languages well. Our weekend class is multilingual and he converses with us easily: in German, Italian and in French. The only language in which his speech is very primitive is mine. I am also the only American there.

Gesturing to me to follow, he takes us up a complicated network of lifts until we reach a sunlit peak where we happily ski up and down a small T-bar slope, exercising our legs, working out the kinks. At lunchtime we sit around a red-checked tablecloth in a small wood mountain hut; and I watch as the others order wine and beer and huge bowls of soup and loaves of bread and chunks of meat covered with a heavy sauce. I restrict myself to soup and coffee. I cannot adjust to European meals; nor do I want to, for I have gone on a program of re-creation; and it is my tubby body I am resculpturing first.

For a little while we sit around. They talk. I get up and go out through the roofed, enclosed entranceway to sit upon an exposed rock. It is lovely and peaceful here. I turn my face to the sun.

Baking, I sit quietly for a while; and, after a long lunchtime rest, the group indolently tumbles out. Groaning at the recharge necessary, we all snap on our skis. The instructor speaks and gestures at me. I follow, and see them all disappearing down a little hill. But as I easily ski behind, I suddenly find them on a narrow path in the middle of an enormous field I did not know was even there. It is piled deeply with unpacked snow, which makes me terribly afraid; for, a few years before in Aspen, I had taken a headfirst fall into this and nearly smothered before

107

someone had come to pull me out. I try to conquer my fear. It is irrational. But I cannot, and tell the skier in front of me to ask the instructor for help. He works his way back up the bowl, stands thigh-deep in the snow, and then places his body directly in front of me so that I will not go sliding wildly, out of control. He speaks in German and, though I do not really know what it is he says, his voice is warm and comforting. They are used to scary girls like me, I think.

Less nervous now, I complete the *piste,* and find the rest of the group waiting at a lift shack like a Gretel cottage, shadowed by huge, black pines, taller than any I have seen before. It is not possible to bend back far enough to see the thin, spiked topmost branches poking through the cloudless sky.

The lift has single chairs. Orderly, taking our places, one by one we board. I am the last, and stand waiting within the raw-wood feeder fence, blotched and dappled by the few spots of sun which manage to penetrate the trees. The lift whirs steadily. I shuffle forward, waiting my turn: calm, but apprehensive at my recent fear. It is a new sensation for me: a mindless panic I could not reason through. It does not matter, I think, as finally my turn comes. I will redeem myself this afternoon. There is not a mountain in the world which is stronger than my will. I have time. I will conquer all of them, one by one, until age and brittling bones finally makes me bow to the one force I must acknowledge superior to my own.

Within the darkling forest, the lift slowly pulls me up and I glide comfortably, suspended among the giant trees whose branches reach, like needled fingertips, almost to the iron towers of German steel.

It is very quiet. There are no voices whooping below, as there are in Vermont; no calling from chair to slope, no shouts of snow euphoria as speeding skiers float off the deep moguls, hypnotized by weightlessness. We are all alone: only the trees and the few seated figures directly in front of me. No one speaks or looks around. Where are we going? Somewhere . . . We will soon find out. For now, we must sit on our moving, suspended chairs and allow ourselves to be taken there. Thought is suspended too: as the smell of pine and shadow and mountain air make tranquil our mysterious ascent among the trees.

Moments pass. I am going up and up. It will soon end, for I can see the sun-break just ahead, at the top of a rounded hill. There is no lift station within sight. It must be just beyond, I think: the slight dip of a runoff where we will leave the chair to begin another downward run.

I open the crossbar, inch forward on the seat, angling my ski tips up, ready to hit the ground again.

With a great arc of straining motion, the machine hauls me over the ridge of the hill.

To find below me: nothingness.

Where am I? What is this? Where have they taken me? I will not go. I must. Sit back. I am suspended over airless space: transported, I am certain of it; unwillingly passed through some matter-disintegrating machine to be reassembled again on an alien planet: on the moon.

We are no longer on the earth. Turn back, turn back. There is some danger threatening here. There is no place on earth like this: an albinoed void: the mutant nightmare of no atmosphere. I cannot breathe.

The line of chairs stretches up in an endless thread of flecked accent marks. The top of it is almost beyond sight, so far away that the tiny figures soldered to the chairs cannot be real. They are like rigid, leaden toys, fixed forever to their seats. The world is bleached, colorless. There are no trees, only a steep angle of white, unbroken except for, far off in the distance, miles below, a small movement which makes S-turns through the snow, like a slowly moving burdened insect: directionless, crawling for home: about to die.

I will not go. Out. Out.

Be still. It is dangerous to move about, to cause motion on the fragile chair.

The world funnels, conically; its access to what I know narrows to a tiny space that might not let me through. And if, ragged and torn, I get through: what then? For eventually when I reach the top I find a spiny ridge with a steep drop-off on either side which

109

I will have to cross before I can begin to ski down. Frightened, terrorized, I am on a balancing wire, trying to keep from falling with two large metal slabs attached to my feet. There is no safety net, and I will go tumbling down and down and down; falling, to land, broken, in some deep crevasse where I will be found, fully preserved, by some futuristic archaeologist excavating the plot before the sealevel homes are built. Female, aged . . . How will they measure time then; or will there be no time, for they will have conquered it? Will they be able to thaw me out, or will I have frozen too slowly for that?

I am petrified. Cautiously I ski into the more gently inclined bowl where our class will begin its descent. My legs are not working properly, and I flop and stutter my way down the slope; forgetting when to lift, forgetting when to bend, sitting back rigid with fear. We reach still another chair, this time a double one, and I find the instructor is waiting to go up with me.

We are developing a pidgin language by now, a kind of semantic internationalism, and converse with an ad-libbed mixture of German, French and English. I gather that what he asks is why I am suddenly skiing so badly, when I did so well in the morning, and there is no powder where we are.

I try to explain: *"La montagne, c'est trop . . . "* switch to German, *"grosse. Ich kanst nicht . . ."* And back, *"J'ai peur."*
"Warum?"

"Je n'ai jamais vue . . ." But somehow, I cannot find the words in any other tongue. I am not even facile in my own, for I do not know how to describe the unearthly feeling I have; nor can I tell this man that I feel as if I am only a slender, dried-out, fragile twig, a bit of lifeless bark; immobile, defenseless. The mountain will come and pick me up and toss me over itself. There is something stronger than I am here. I am unimportant, without worth. It is more powerful than anything I have ever met before; and I am more unimportant, more worthless than I have ever been: a bit of human scrap. I can be discarded easily.

A thrombosis has occurred: paralyzed and helpless, I must leave myself in the mountain's hands. I am afraid.

And here, recalling, my mind blanks out; for I can remember

nothing after that except for a brief flash of sunlight between the trees as we made our way down in the late afternoon. I do not remember coming down. I do not remember being down, or returning to my hotel. What I remember is that I went to sleep. I did not ski the next day, but wandered among the Sunday-deserted streets, ate lunch and dinner and went back to sleep again. I did not investigate the après-ski life. There would be time for that. I was tired. The jets had caught up with me. I slept, wiping the mountain out; I slept, huddled under the billowing Austrian comforter with two down pillows at my head and my small travel clock ticking, its hands and numerals glowing neon green in the dark. I slept, I drew the drapes; for, outside my window, the mountain reached down almost to the building where I was. I drew the drapes and slept. I will get used to it. I can get used to anything. It all takes time.

I nurse myself. I am placed within a class run by a thin, lithe blond who laughs a lot and flirts in front of us; who teases an English girl with roseate skin. "Bar-bara, Bar-bara," he chants her name. "Bar-bara with the long dark hair." Rapunzel. She blushes. I study him, standing at Barbara's side: wondering what the difference is; and why is it I am invisible again?

We do not lunch together. The instructor has other concerns, and I see him circling the bar at the bottom of the slope. I eat alone, seated at tables of strangers who all seem to know each other, who cross the giant room to stop and talk and chatter in a babel of languages. There is a family with a little girl: the parents are European, the girl is an Asian. She is not two feet high and waddles around up and down the aisles in a jumbo snowsuit while her father runs after her and swoops her up and she laughs at him as he carries her back slung over his shoulder, holding her firmly and passionately.

I hear talk. In France there has been an avalanche. I wish to know how many lived. I hear the word for death in many languages. That is a word I know, though I can really speak no other tongue than my own. I do not ask. I will not intrude. There is a privacy here I cannot overcome.

I eat alone; and after skiing wander through the shopping ar-

111

cades of Kitzbühel, finding nothing to buy. The prices are like those in the States. There are no bargains anymore for rich Americans like me.

I drink afternoon chocolate with a paperback in front of me. I speak to no one. No one speaks to me, comes over, sits down, asks me my name and who I am and how long will I stay and will you have dinner with me tonight?

I eat alone, dressing every evening in the flossy après-ski clothes of Sugarbush with the silver-buttoned coat I have especially bought. The waiters seat me at little tables; on crowded evenings I share, but only with other women, most of whom are elderly. I order my half liter of wine, drink it all, and go to bed.

It is no use. There is something wrong. I attend a tea dance and no one speaks to me except for one young German who shrugs his shoulders and then walks away. I am baffled by the barrier. Don't they all speak English?

I offer chocolate to a couple on the slopes. I am refused. What's happening here? Member of a conquering nation, am I ignored in the land that my own virtue has won for me? I am an American . . . American! Still I spend every night alone. We are outnumbered here. I rarely hear an American voice or see, in the streets, that particular kind of face that marks people of my own outward-bred native land: the fine, clean lines that are an intermingling of the fresh genetic material that has made my country so fiercely great.

They are crippled by their history: by the rapes and pillagings and the armies which have marched back and forth over their lands, leaving only bombed ruins and the stench of decay. Impotent people, where would you be without my care? If you prosper now it is because of me. If you are alive it is only because I saved bits of soap and scraps of tin and sewed tiny garments for your young who now walk up and down the streets, shouldering their skis, their ski boots sounding on the cobbled roads; who now, tall and well fed and muscled and with steel-gray eyes, are all ignoring me.

Is this how you return the pennies of my youth, to cast me out as if I were a ragged, fetid doll you have dirtied with misuse?

112

Weeks of dull misery wrap themselves around me and finally send me out one night to an icy odyssey among the primeval streets. Isolated, tremblingly alone, I enter a dark alley and suddenly see words written there on an ancient, iced-blue wall.

"You are a bunch of . . ." What I mean to say is "Nazis." What comes out is "Niggers!" It is all different now. No one wants me anymore. I am not adored. Niggers! That's the word. "They're all niggers!"

From on high, Baldwin's words flash like a retributive finger of light. . . . "I know that you invented him because you needed him." Followed by a deafening roar:

"Who is the nigger here?"

Through the streets of Kitzbühel, the resounding gurgle of Teutonic laughter follows me. *I* am the nigger here! A generation ago they invented me because they needed me. But now *I* have invented *them!*

Through the preserved film archives of the Reich, I have put myself within the camps of Auschwitz, Dachau and of Belsen. Part of the camera's eye, I have panned down the marketplace of Guernica, past figures of little girls, obscenely sprawled, clutching bloodied dolls, victims of the Condor passes. Trucking shots have taken me through the lined avenues of Paris, sound tracks recording the rumbling of tanks and the sobs of that immortal Frenchman who was not ashamed to cry. And from outside the walls of Warsaw, telephoto lenses caught in sharp detail the explosions of my people as they were returned to dust.

Yet there have been other wars that I have also lived in this century where everything is recorded and preserved until the nitrated chemicals call back the images to dust again:

—hoses play on marchers in Selma; a cavalry charge of lawmen, nightsticks raised;

—tanks rumble down the manicured mall, cameras sweeping up to reveal nests of machine guns set on the marbled parapets of Washington, D.C.;

—blood on the streets of Chicago; nightsticks and flame in Newark; in New York and Saigon, human torches crumble on the sidewalks; and in Vietnam, the pilots are peeled from their seats like burnt marshmallows whose soft insides have liquefied, seeping through charred outer skin with a pustular stickiness.

Selma is not Auschwitz, Chicago not Guernica, Washington not Paris. Newark is *different* than Warsaw. How? I am not sure. I have viewed it all in blazing Ektachrome, this history of man, now looped in the film of my shining land. My country has blasted me from belief, for I have seen American megalomania betray its own childish creed. We are all murderers. Then . . . I, too, could kill.

The chants of children overpower me.

"The boogeyman will get you if you don't watch out."

But I have watched, and now the niggers do. Rap Brown or Poitier? Unknowing, they battle for my soul, ranged against each other, and against me too, in a deadly conflict of disciplines.

I find it is both their voices that I carry with me into another week. They are louder now and will not be ignored. I have been transferred to a more expert class; and now it is death I meet on the side of an Austrian Alp.

The barking voice of the ski instructor, weathered by middle age, rings out at me. "Come here," he commands. "You are stupid to be so afraid."

But I am, again, paralyzed by fear. We have skied on a narrow ledge, circling a distant side of the monumental range, miles away from all the lifts. Inexperienced with this kind of terrain, lacking any warning of our destination, I do not know and have not been taught how to stop a swiftening descent. I am terrified. The instructor is many yards away. He does not move to place his body between me and the plummeting cliff that is like the steep side of a bottomless bowl. Instead, he summons me to plunge straight down into the heavy powder snow.

I have noticed his leathered, blunted fingers, nails clipped in a straight line at the tip. Like a film loop, my obsessive dream— repeated since childhood—plays and replays; jackboots echoing beside a caravan of railroad cars. I have tried all day not to be afraid of him. But I still cannot control my fear of this kind of snow. I cannot breathe. I will suffocate. I cannot forget. If I fall, I will die before he can plow his way up—in deliberate slow

114

motion—from the bottom of the precipice.

The rest of the class is embarrassed by me. I am the only American here. They too, they confide, are afraid. But one by one, in order, down they go. Impossible American, only I refuse.

"You must do as he says," one of the women calls to me.

"Why must I?" Sobbing, as much with anger as with fear, I pack the snow down for myself in a crossways trail, making another path; and coolly apply a trained intellect to finding a circuitous route through the dangerous forest where I must make my way independently and alone. Strangely, as carefully I plot my *piste*, sighting by the semaphoric shafts of sun which occasionally pierce through the gigantic trees, I have become very calm. I have refused to go, but I find no shame in me; nor do I feel I have disgraced my nation on this international stage. "You must do as he says." My answer has been an automatic "Why?" It is, I realize, the difference between their nations and mine. In spite of what Stokely says—

"the total white America . . . is incapable of condemning herself for the acts of brutality and bestiality she's heaped upon the black community . . . "

in Rap Brown's Reich we turn our cameras on ourselves, and flick our sets in nightly recognition of our own horrors. Is it our people who must be herded with guns and bayonets into a recognition of our camps? What else was Chicago, '68, but the clash of ideologies open on the streets? And it was the satellites we had made which communicated our murders to the world.

We are a nation of molecular dimension whose implosions create evolutionized elements which have not yet found their neatly numbered ways onto the scientific charts: a form of life rending itself into a thousand parts in a national reproduction of survival strengths. We recombine ourselves through testing, through experiment. Through facing pain. Nobody tells us what we must do; for we always ask "Why must I?" And we can also shout "I will not!" and willingly pay the price of risks taken independently; though we are still afraid. We can be alone, and have the ability to face ourselves and see what is is that we are.

Slowly, in agony, we outgrow our need for niggers, for the

reference point of a lower order in order to qualitatively define ourselves; in order to prove we are better, stronger, more intelligent: omnipotent, therefore invulnerable; therefore immortal too. We cannot die. We can. But we can also fight for our lives . . . and with mortal chance, sometimes also win.

Late that afternoon, exhausted but at peace, I find the group—bloodied by their self-inflicted fatigue—in a tiny bierstube set in the base of the mountain. They jabber about me in German, confident I don't understand. But I have been hearing Yiddish all my life, and so I understand enough to catch the phrase "Let's get rid of her." They need not worry. Tomorrow, I have decided, I will board a train. I am returning home from Europe; an American tourist again, now learned from Europe much more than Europe thought to teach. An American anger has preserved my life: I am woman, contemporary, American. Poitier has won. Where is safety and defense? It is in myself. And pride in myself has eliminated the need for fantasies which keep me floating above the roiling, murderous earth.

I am woman, contemporary, American. I no longer need to be omnipotent too; and becoming human at last, I have lost the fear of my own anger. "Kill or be killed," they said. Afraid that I could —and would—I had given up feeling because it was too dangerous; and giving up multiplies itself. "Kill or be killed." I need not kill to preserve my life. There is another way. I am, now, allowed to feel. (They applauded him.) Feeling is life, not death.

I am woman, contemporary, American. Perhaps I am an artist too. Is it possible, that particular dream?

In Kitzbühel, the lights begin to glow in the chalets, restaurants and coffee shops. Shouldering my skis, I use my poles as walking sticks as I thread my way along the cobbled narrow streets. I am very hungry; too hungry to shower, dress and then go out. I will have dinner in my room tonight. Besides, I am to leave tomorrow. I have a great deal to do. I must: (1) call through to Munich, arranging for my flight; (2) check train schedules outward bound; (3) settle my bill; (4) gather up the belongings which are scattered through my room and pack them all carefully away; (5) get a good night's rest so that I will be fresh and unfatigued for the long journey home.

Mentally, I make a schedule, setting aside time for every task. It is necessary to be efficient, faced with multiplicity. An imposed order will simplify.

Between today and tomorrow there is not much time.

Book Three

The Casualties of War

1

The last days of winter sit softening on the land. I get up a little earlier now, to walk to work, leisurely winding through the forest paths of Central Park; noticing as, day by day, the seasons change; as the incubated forms of life begin thrusting through the replenished soil. They are still fragile, tentative, delicately stalked. It is early yet. There will be time.

Adam Clayton Powell stands just ahead. He is a showman whose satined theatrics have always attracted me. But, I discover as I return to work, the theatrics rest on a solid thematic base. There is a natural tension in what he says. The play is undeniable.

I find him in several different places, in several different rolls of film: on the polished floor of a university gymnasium, addressing the balcony; and sitting at a stage-platform desk, where the light picks him up against a velvet ground. On both sets, the thrust of his speech is the same.

"Black is not the color of your skin," he says to me. "Black is the way you think. We're thinking the same as an Italian, an Irishman, a Pole or a Jew. In other words, there are a lot of you out there who can think black and still be white."

121

Thinking black: what does that mean?

"Now black power was first originated when I was twelve years old by a semiliterate black man from Jamaica named Marcus Garvey."

I have to smile at the invocation. It is an apt example for Powell to use; for Garvey—among all the other things he was—was the consummate showman too.

"Marcus Garvey never preached anti-white because he who is against anyone is against himself."

I know. James Baldwin taught me that.

"He never preached violence because . . . when you're in an argument the person who strikes the first blow has confessed they've lost the argument.

"Black power," he continues to define, "is merely an attempt at equality of dignity, an equality of character, and equality of recognition by nonblacks of our negritude."

And that I am woman, contemporary, American. That I will—perhaps—be artist too.

"We are proud of the fact that we are black. This means that we want to be called black.

"It means that we're not anti-white. But we're pro-black.

"It means that we do not believe in violence. But we do not believe in total nonviolence.

"We are not aggressors. But we are defenders."

And "I will not!" I answer them.

"It means we have black dignity, black integrity and we want black equality.

"We're proud of this nation. We want to belong to it. We want a piece of the action. We have been waiting three hundred years for it. And we're going to get it. We're going to get it, we hope, nonviolently. We're going to get it one way or the other.

"And we want it now.

"Now.

"Now!"

Ah, Adam, it's not yet time. And we both shall have to wait a little longer for recognition of our negritude. It all takes time. We must be patient. We must wait. Change does not come forcefully.

122

But for Powell there had been no more time. When I view this, he is congressman no more; and listening to him I sadly remember the bluster I had seen on a television talk show. Challenged, finally he backed down.

"I've paid my dues," he said. "I've paid my dues."

Carefully selecting, taking notes, paper-tabbing the film, I rewind to the beginning, heads up, wondering if giving up is the same as giving in; and wondering, too, how to tell when enough credits have accrued to earn a lifetime membership in the state. Did he know he was dying then?

One day, interrupting my work on the black series to research a film about the March on Washington, I suddenly stumble across a man whose name, at the time, I do not even bother to note. (Later, going back, I find the camera report sheet with a scribbled note. It says only "...a Mr. Sharpe.") He is not a black celebrity. But there is something in his voice that slows my hand from rolling quickly past his speech.

He is seated at a highly polished witness table, before a bank of microphones. In the front of the room, on a raised dais, sit the congressional judges who have come to solemnly hear the pleas. Softly, quietly, Mr. Sharpe speaks:

> They say we are apes, monkeys . . . less than human.
> But I know I am as great as any white man
> that ever lived and ever will live.
> We want to create like the white race creates
> because we are a creative people.
> We just don't want to be the bricklayer.
> We want to be the designer,
> the architect.
> We just don't want to be the pilot of the plane.
> We want to be the designer of the plane.
> Do you understand what I'm trying to say?

No. But I hear.

> These are the things that we feel.
> These are the things that we know we have to do. . . .
> We have to establish our identity.

We have to regain back our culture.
We have to get our stolen heritage.
These things have been denied us too long
    as people. . . .

We are hungry.
We're starving.
We're crying inside.
And white America refuses to hear.

I hear. I hear. But what does it mean? I have been through the Long March of your people; and I, too, have begun to mourn. But in this land of freedom, what guilt is mine, whose family history includes slavery and genocide in *this* century?

But if I have not, truly, understood your words, for having heard the argument too many times before, I have now heard something else. I have heard your music: a faint melody, derivative perhaps, but shaped by your recital of it into a furtherance of form, an extension of principles long since become classic: compacted, molded, reshaped in your pressure-cooked black mind until it is no longer a verbal symphony presented, once removed, upon a stage where it can be viewed with safety. I do not understand. But you have, somehow, involved me in the tragedy of your life. Black Everyman—Stagolee—had you, somewhere, heard Shylock speak?

Enraptured by Sharpe's voice, I bring the film with me to the office, recommending its use. But Everyman has no place in our black box. Sharpe is refused; and, sadly, I bring him back to the film library and return him to the high-racked, bulging vault. A new age of oratory has begun, I think. Unrecognized, ignored as new forms often are, still it is a great aural literature. Uneducated, inarticulate people, have you, unnoticed, brought to this deadened world your own powerful poetry?

Could one of your poets be . . . Bobby Seale?

From deep within the jungle, now I hear the Panther's roar:

We—ell,

he flutes, eyes half-closed, hearing his own arpeggios of sound,

> what's it all about,
> fire?
> They say fire's supposed to stop
> fire.
> I say fire don't stop
> fire.
> I say the only thing to put out fire is
> water!
> And the only way you can put out fire is with
> a bunch of,
> a bunch of
> people!

Swaying,

> Well,
> I say,
> a bunch of
> pee-ee-pull!

I have leaned into the viewer, head nodding in the ancient chant song of those who stand, in genetic procession, for five millennia inside of me. Bobby Seale, then still an advocate of "the gun as a proper, a *very* proper revolutionary tool." Yet he is mine. In the actions of worship, we unite. And are all gods not the same? Only forms are different. His is the gun. And mine?

> If white folks is going to play Nazis,
> black folks ain't going to play Jews.

Even Jews no longer play Jews. Israel is my survival now. I *can* fight. And sometimes win.

But, still puzzled, as I type within my whitewashed room where the sun stays longer and grows stronger every day, I wonder what is the way to win? The hostilities of H. Rap Brown bring only deadly counterattack. And Poitier's righteous anger says "Don't tread on me." Or else. But I am small and fragile; and, though righteous anger is a defense for me too, still it is a defense of negatives. For what it calls for is a lonely and dangerous journey through a forest. All alone.

Is there another way? Shall I always have to isolate myself to fight my wars? Do the internalized conflicts of my country mean a disregard for other human beings because there is no time, no energy for giving elsewhere; because there is only time and energy enough to keep from giving up?

Do we have to give up everything else in order to survive ourselves?

But now, on the quickening track, comes the sound of another voice. The Reverend Ralph David Abernathy, preaching to his people in their native tongue: a Passion in the Black Vernacular:

> Thanks be to God, the Eternal Being,
> who stepped out from nowhere into Somewhere
> and spoke in the midst of darkness
> and there was light.
> Oceans began to flow.
> Streams came into being.
> Plants began to bloom.
> I'm talking about a God.
> Do you know Him?

Shoulders heaving, he tells us all:

> If you're burdened down,
> He's a burden-bearer.
> If your heart is wrong,
> He's a heart-fixer.
> If your mind is disturbed,
> He's a mind-regulator.

Again he asks:

> Do you know Him?

The fervor of response fills the room. Free, joyous, shouting . . . unrestricted. A litany of faith responsive to the combustible

126

poetry of love. A thousand miles away in space, and months removed in time, I, too, want to join, shouting my belief. What belief? I am a relapsed everything. Against the deadly gases long ago I masked myself. It is impossible to separate the fumes of hate and love, death and life. I have denied them all. Defenses multiply themselves. I have given up . . . everything.

The old psalms return:

"The Lord is my shepherd; I shall not want. He maketh me to lie down in green pastures: he leadeth me beside the still waters."

The new land bears strange, rich fruits.

"Thou preparest a table before me in the presence of mine enemies. . . ."

There is comfort here in the faiths of love, and the beatitudes of peace here too.

"Yea, though I walk through the valley of the shadow of death, I will fear no evil: for thou art with me. . . ."

Continuing my journey, one day upon the road I meet the burbling, joyous figure of Muhammad Ali, addressing an outdoor meeting of college students on a campus just upstate. The fighter, the sportsman's golden boy, socks it to his audience as Dick Gregory once did.

"The black man has been brainwashed and it's time for him to learn something about himself.

"He look at television, he see:

"White Owl cigars, white Swan soap, White Rain hair rinse, White Tornado floor wax, White-Plus toothpaste.

"They taught him when he was a little boy that:

"Mary had a little lamb whose feet was white as snow. Then they taught him about Snow White. Then there's the White House.

"When he look at television he sees two cars, one black and one white. And they put a gallon of gas in each one and see which one can go the farest. Every time the black car stop first and the white car keep goin'.

"Brainwashes the Negroes.

"Then he goes to the drugstore and orders two dips ice cream. He say I want a dip-a-chocolate and a dip-a-vanilla, and every

127

time they put the chocolate on the bottom and the vanilla on the top!

". . . When he goes to the grocery store, he goes to get cake, he sees an angel food cake is the white cake and the devil food cake is the chocolate cake.

"Everything bad is black. So he's been brainwashed. He needs to be taught something about himself so he can be proud. . . .

"It's our job to rebrainwash him that:

"Rich bread is black bread. Strong coffee is black coffee."

The audience is laughing agreeably. "Don't feel bad," he tells the white faces in the crowd.

"So now he feels proud, he's not beggin' you no more. No. He's glad to be hisself, he's not worryin' you anymore. . . ."

Drawing himself up, he says:

"Any intelligent people love their history. Chinese love their beautiful culture and are not seeking to lose their identity. Puerto Ricans love their beautiful culture. Mexicans love their beautiful culture. And the white man love his. Because I see wagon trains on television every day. And stagecoaches.

"We're not seeking to lose our identity in blood mixing. And our beautiful black African history.

"We don't hate you. We don't hate those of you who are white. We just want to stay black.

"We love our color.

"I just love myself!"

Love. Champ. I would like to meet that man. Hi, Champ. I love you. But I would not say the words. I could not. Love is gone from my vocabulary. Love is a word I never say anymore.

"We don't hate those of you who are white. We just want to stay black. We love our color. I just love myself!"

But I do hate. I hate those who would take my life from me. Still, in defense of myself, I need not kill, convinced of my own regnancy. I can hate and still stay alive. Therefore, there is no need to hate myself for feeling hate. But if I can feel hate, allow myself to rage, is it possible that feeling multiplies itself? Is it possible I could feel . . . something else? That I could . . . love the nigger who lives inside of me?

128

"Black is not the color of your skin. Black is the way you think." Am I becoming black within? The synonym for black: is it love? Carrying the excitement with me, I have dinner with the Austrian, to whom I had spoken once again at a club meeting in a German restaurant. Conversationally at first, I had told him of journeying to Kitzbühel. We had been standing at the bar, his back turned to the high, vinyled bumper against which he leaned, arms folded in front of him. Conscious of who—and what —we both were, I did not tell him everything: not history, but only of the threatening mountain, the loneliness and isolation there. He listened carefully, face registering no reaction, but Mongol eyes never leaving my face to wander, flickering restlessly about the room as the club membership shifted, never still: exchanging greetings, a few words. Then moving on.

The Austrian remained with me. He said nothing as I talked for quite a while. And then, offering me his arm, had driven me home in his powerful, shining American car. I had wondered at his hidden perceptions, remembering: "You are so tame now," wondering if he knew, for I did not, why I had been that way. I had been secretly watching him, noticing an inexplicable monastic quality that often occurred, like the sudden, swift lifting of a bridge over which he walked so freely at other times; when, at other times, observing the club après-ski life, he commently wryly, "We all have too much grease on us," and, laughing at looped antics, said, "They stone themselves."

But he also seemed to draw away repeatedly, grimly, from others as well as from myself. It was a quality to which I could not react. I, myself, had led a cellular life for many years, love packed away like a decapitated doll among the fairy-tale books with broken spines. It was a long time ago, when I was very, very young. I had neither forgotten nor forgiven. Life consisted of a series of going-ons.

But now, at dinner, I tell him of my adventure into this black world, and of the great and beautiful discoveries within. He is as moved as I am by the hidden, sonorous sounds as I recite them over the evening music of the small restaurant. He listens with an intensity I find profoundly affecting. This, too, is new to me.

I have never seen this in anyone before.

Deeply we discuss: "What is black?" He has read a story in *The New York Times* about Israeli law, and we link up—together—the corollaries of our conversation: "What is a Jew?" I have had too much to drink, perhaps, for suddenly I begin to tell him what I have never before discussed. Glass shatters and skulls crack as I describe the hegira of my family, moved about through centuries of pogrom, self-severed finally and irrevocably from our homeland. To escape conscription, a great-uncle cut off his thumb. The Czar's troops came to take a brother in his place. Through an aging aunt, I heard of my grandmother's childhood tears as her father was led away.

I come, finally, to that single letter received long after the war from a distant cousin who was the only one left. Leaning over the fine dinner cloth, I am unable to stop keening over that anonymous trench in the wilderness of Russia, the inner music constantly within: "They say we are apes, monkeys . . . less than human." Transposed to English words, it is still the Hebrew lament: a Kaddish in perpetuity.

I am too much aware of the irony here. Our fathers, had they met, would have had to kill each other. In a way they did. Both engineers, his was building railroads while mine was building ships. And in our childhoods, had we been able to view each other across that sea, we would have shouted hate: flinging epithets like rocks. "Die, die," I would have shouted in the untended field. And he would have sought my death too: "Die, die!" And brought me bleeding to the ground.

Not now, however: not on this enchanted evening. He has become my first Austrian. I am his first Jew. He has heard my agony and now I hear his answering pain.

"Why do they always kill the Jews?"

We talk of war and death and hate, and I hear how it was on the other side during those years when I was collecting scraps of soap and saving tons of tin.

"We never starved," he says first. And to my further question also says, "Ah, the Russians . . . It was not so bad."

I wonder at that too.

Life, however, was not all calm, all rural peace. Deep in Russia, his father had deserted after Stalingrad and somehow made his way back home. The SS tracked him down.

"I still hear my mother scream," he says, calmly.

"What did they do?"

"They put him in a camp. He had to take apart the mines."

"Were you frightened?"

"Frightened?" He pauses, as if to question his own memory. "Ah, no. I was just a little boy. I knew he would return to us."

Not frightened by your mother's screams? Saying nothing, I merely nod.

Filled with music and with wine, we return to my apartment, where he seats himself upon the couch, under the laden bookshelves, among the paintings and old copper and little collections that I love.

"It is very nice here. It is very comfortable," he says, leaning back, settling in. And, as men and women inevitably do on enchanted evenings such as this, we begin to talk of more recent history, of feelings and of where they lead.

He feels nothing, he says. Past thirty, he has never been "involved," though he is able to flesh the skeleton I have packed away. "Pain," he counsels quietly, "is part of growing up." Quizzically, I throw the statement back and see him, leaning forward, elbows on his knees, trying to find the words with which to explain inexplicable pressures within. Almost to himself he says, "I get . . . I cannot breathe. You understand. It is a kind of claustrophobia. I run away from it."

Understanding, I gather up our glasses and in the kitchen stand wrestling with a tray of ice. It is unyielding, for the cubes have remained there for quite a while. I have had little use for them. Heritage forbids it. I never drink alone.

There is silence in the other room while I am away: the silence of European mourning, of facing pain, of enduring, perhaps. "Perhaps all of these indignities of war have left wounds which will take time to heal and infinite patience to understand."

"Do you know what a phobia comes from?" I ask, returning, curling up on the couch next to him.

"No," he answers, looks at me, waits for me to speak, to explain something to him.

I explain to him that a phobia is an unreasonable, irrational fear. There is no real danger threatening; it only seems that way. It comes from a time of childhood, when all dangers are all too real. It comes from an inability to distinguish, an inability to separate the present from the childhood threat. It comes from never having learned, as somehow most children do, how to handle the concept of their own ultimate annihilation: that, in time, death always comes. Death, too, is part of growing up.

Thinking of the war, I ask, "Were you ever close to death?"

He leans back against the couch, staring at the large painting of the sea on the opposite wall. All my paintings are of water and of ships somehow.

"Yes," he says.

But it is not a war story that he tells, but of a summertime after, when, one day, he and a younger brother camped in a forest at the edge of a large lake. The room darkens as he speaks. There is only his voice: a brushed whisper: a soliloquy.

"I was perhaps twelve, thirteen then," he says. "I do not remember exactly. The water was very cold, but I am a good swimmer and I go far out into the lake. It is very beautiful. There is no one. Just us. The forest is quiet. There is no one on the lake. I turn to go back. I am getting cold, tired. But I cannot get back to shore. Something is pulling me away. Some kind of . . . from beneath the water. It takes me away. And I see where it carries me. There is a kind of . . ."

He motions with his hands: a waterfall, he means.

"The lake, it ends. There is machinery. Dangerous. I get very, very close to it. It has like . . . spikes. I know if I fall in . . . ah, that is the end of me."

"What did you do?"

Turning, he smiles. The lights come back up again. "Well, you see, I am still here."

"How did you get away? You were so tired by that time."

"I see the machinery, I forget how tired I am. I swim like hell." Chuckling, remembering, he shakes his head.

132

"Is that when the claustrophobia began?" I ask.

He shrugs his shoulders. "I do not remember. But when we go camping again, I will not let my brother close the tent. He makes a lot of shouting. It is cold at night. But the tent stays open or I do not go with him again."

I understand. Sadly, I understand too much. Wrapped in his émigré world, the Austrian has not been pried out of it, as I have, by the prodding of Julian Bond, who has also recently taken his place in the growing messianic chorus of blacks whose voices are now always part of my inner dialogues. It is the wisdom of Snick that Bond proclaims on the films I have just recently seen.

". . . in some parts of the South white people are willing and eager to kill Negroes. . . . You have to be careful. But you can't allow yourself to become paralyzed by fear."

They wish to exercise the right to vote. My needs are even more basic: I wish simply to exercise my right to the fullness of life: contemporary, American. Perhaps artist too. The component parts of a state of being called womanhood. Thus, black wisdom counsels me, I must force myself to use again those severed muscles atrophied by fear. It will cost me much agony, but slowly the paralysis will disappear.

". . . time to heal and infinite patience to understand . . ."

Thus, patiently, I set myself on an after-hours research into the Austrian musculature. I wish to see his world as he saw it then, to know how it felt to live in that time when, both children, we were enemies. With infinite patience I track down library catalog cards, but all I find are the reports of our side. Until one day I stumble upon *Night Falls on the City,* by Sarah Gainham, the first of a trilogy of novels set in Austria; and I read of the "horror of loneliness" and of the weapons it provides:

"This control . . . is based on what must be the deepest fear of human beings—to be alone, driven out, isolated from their own kind. People will do anything to avoid that. . . . Freud has it all wrong. What dominates human beings is this fear of being left alone and it comes from the long helplessness of human childhood when to be abandoned means death. . . . This is the sure instinct of madmen, that they have picked on this fear. What else were these camps but places where men ceased to exist, never were?"

Abandoned by the world, we marched together, huddled close: instinctively madmen knew our fear.

". . . black folks ain't going to play Jews . . ."

they are going to scatter, spread themselves among us.

". . . the only way you can put out fire is with
a bunch of,
a bunch of
people!"

who will all cling together finding, among their own kind, a place, a verdant Oz, where fresh, clear

"Streams came into being," and

"Plants began to bloom."

Do you know him? Not yet. I am still looking: my researches carrying me into books of myself. I follow Sarah Gainham's trilogy to *A Place in the Country,* where I read this description of a young Austrian girl:

"It was clear that nothing of the terrible kind of [Russian] savagery we heard all too much of ever happened, for [they] even joked about their tricks and ruses of evasion. . . . But the strain and wariness left in her a kind of emotional lassitude that she never quite lost. . . ."

And in *Private Worlds,* the last:

"It was, the whole period and its black emotions, an artifically induced psychoneurosis. . . . And he went on to surmise the pervasive mass psychoneurosis still smothering great tracts of Europe in its breathless pall. [He] thought of this pall as a future endemic social danger, the danger of spontaneous explosions of rage."

The winds of atmosphere revolve, carrying clouds of ash across the seas, to other continents, where social danger becomes endemic and the symptoms are spontaneous bursts of social rage.

But the Austrian is very quiet. He never raises his voice. There is a gentleness in him that is, to me, an unfamiliar quality in a male. Sadly, the Austrian asks:

"Why do they always kill the Jews?"

Austrian, I suspect that you, too, will try.

"I cannot breathe. I run away from it."

In your own defense, with quiet black rage, you will turn your weapons on me.

> We are hungry.

> We're starving.

> And white America refuses to hear.

But I am now comforted by the visionary voices who teach me not to be afraid. I have weapons of my own, and I will fight: finding my voice. Cut and bruised by black, there is a reward for having made the swim.

I see it. I see you.

Holding your hand, can I induce you to test the glacial waters once again? Will you journey with me upon the glimmering road to Oz?

There is danger, but it seems so simple. Patience and understanding. "It all takes time." I will wait a little longer, until you are a little stronger.

In America, all dreams come true. Behind the screen, the music of Romeo and Juliet plays on. For me, forever, the song of love.

⤚ 2

Spring. Nature's rising heat begins to ferment the processes of the heart. The land becomes new-green. Knee-deep, I am wandering with childhood wonder; lifting my face to the sun; stooping often to examine, to touch, to smell; to impress upon my mind, like bouquets we wish forever to preserve, what I find in this golden journey I am taking into the world of black. "In the safety and freedom of the therapeutic relationship," I am becoming my tenderness.

I have been, however, too long entwined with rolls of film. Exploring almost everything in the files, from an initial list of forty names I have selected the most meaningful of twenty differing philosophies: for we have uncovered a whole spectrum of black thought we never recognized was there and this has now become the series framework for which I searched, back in the beginning of time.

But I have paid for our structure, and my therapy, with a loss of visual objectivity. Laocoön-like, I am caught by twisted celluloid raveled around. It is impossible to put everything neatly back. For a while my eyes will be useless. The images, confusing, have strung themselves in my mind like the notes of a music

136

score. I still cannot link them up. It is time to put an end to viewing. It is time to reflect on what I've seen.

Another process begins. I am asked to do a biography for each of the twenty films: a teachers' guide. Writing will serve as an antidote, a period of rest while my vision returns.

Sunlight pours in through that part of the window not blocked by the air-conditioner. The white office cubicle is very bright with it. I find it difficult to begin: my typewriter is caked with disuse. Searching for a new path, in this way I embark upon another journey. For in the world of secret books, I am to discover the terrible cathartic structure of a culture long hidden from my plundering world. I enter the throbbing territory of the black mind; and, in an unknowing upheaval, disgorge safety forever from my life.

Begin at the beginning now: with Abernathy. Looking for a lead, I discover the institution of the black church, described in *The Negro Revolt,* by Louis Lomax:

"Whenever a people are isolated—by choice or by force, to a limited or total extent—they develop a folkway. In classical cultural terms, there is no difference between the Negro Baptist Church and the Baptist Church proper. In folk terms, however, there is. Not only do we Negro Baptists have a way of preaching and singing, but there is a meaning to our imagery that is peculiar to us."

It is a ritual observed secretly: the countercode to madmen who play upon the isolate fear.

"After all, a theology is the result of man's groping with adverse powers . . . and the function of a gospel is to speak to the frustrations of the people who espouse it."

Outwardly conforming to white theology, the black church has developed rooting branches of its own. Segregated, penned like animals, it tells its celebrants, "You are a child of the King." There is no blue-eyed Jesus here. The image has changed, and with it the language too: a thunderous and affecting liturgy develops from the black folkways of expressive love.

There is another version of King James. Long before, hungering for theological truth, I had read *The Passover Plot.* And now I wonder once again: was the self-fulfilling prophet King?

Piecing together the rise of Julian Bond, I find this description of gospel's civil arm in an article by John Neary in *Life* magazine:

". . . tearing around the South in Snick's distinctive whip-antennaed Plymouth Savoys . . . 'This is Zero-one, calling Zero-two; I'm 50 miles from Sunflower, and coming in, VAROOM!' There were midnight chases by the police, with daring 'moonshiner turns'—lights out, a hard left U-turn on a dirt road, the brakes almost locked, a touch of the emergency brake, a double-clutch down into low, and the gas pedal flat—to career back past the policemen there wondering, 'Where'd he go, where'd he go?' "

The constant split screen juxtaposes images recalled by Hollywood's child: on one side, through the Nazi night of 1944, the French underground slips past the German war machines; and on the other, what I see is Mississippi, 1964. Born in 1940, Bond was still too young for our picture shows. Are underground fighters always the same? I had not known that midnight chases with armed police were happening in the land of the free.

I must write a biography of Rap Brown too. His book is mnemonically terrible. Its title is *Die, Nigger, Die!* It abrades the self-exposing surfaces of my life, as he himself has done. Reading, I find, however, my essential opinion of him remains unchanged. He has written a testament of hate. Beneath his reasoning is a case history like a psychology text. And though, sadly, I have come to understand his Reichian view, the emotions it arouses in him are still, to me, the product of a mind made irrecoverably irrational.

Yet, among the twisted arguments, I find another sort of man: the poet of tragedy. There is a street game of which I have never heard, played by children denied access to the printed word. Signifyin' is "a way of expressing your feelings," Rap Brown writes:

> "Man, I can't win for losing.
> If it wasn't for bad luck,
> I wouldn't have no luck at all.

138

I been having buzzard luck.
Can't kill nothing and won't nothing die.. . .
I don't feel no pain.
But it's your world.. . .
If I had your hands I'd give 'way both my arms
'cause I could do without them."

And the trumpeting folk song of black manhood. "We played the Dozens for recreation like white folks play Scrabble."

"I'm the man who walked the water and tied the whale's tail
in a knot
taught the little fishes how to swim
crossed the burning sands and shook the devil's hand . . .
used a Cobra snake for a necktie
And got a brand new house on the roadside made from a
cracker's hide,
got a brand new chimney sitting on top made from the
cracker's skull
Took a hammer and nail and built the world and calls it
'The Bucket of Blood'. . .
I roam the world I'm known to wander and this .45 is
where I get my thunder.

I'm the only man in the world who knows why white milk
makes yellow butter."

Crippled, man turns to a compensatory beauty. Searching, following some instinctive, unregulated track being laid out for me, I dip into history to find this quoted description by Sir Francis Bacon in Catherine Drinker Bowen's book *The Lion and the Throne*. Shrewdly, Bacon writes of his malformed adversary Robert Cecil:

"Whosoever hath any thing fixed in his person that doth induce contempt, hath also a perpetual spur in himself to rescue and deliver himself from scorn. Therefore all deformed persons are extreme bold. First, as in their own defense . . . but in process of time by a general habit. Also it stirreth in them industry, and especially of this kind, to watch and observe the weakness of others, that they may have somewhat to repay. Again, in their superiors, it quencheth jealousy towards them, as persons that they think they may at pleasure despise; and it layeth their competitors and emulators asleep; as never believing they should be in possibility of advancement, till they see them in possession."

H. Rap Brown, whom I despise, takes possession of my images: I am deformed too: female-fragile, isolated and alone: invisible. I am ignored, my gifts refused. Are they sleeping? Is there a way to wake them up? Aroused, what will they do to me then? Is excellence to be encouraged, a quality which is much prized? Or is excellence only a danger which ignites, since superiors see in the possibility of my advancement that which will cripple them: and they need the definition of my lower order in order to define themselves?

I have no answers to these questions with which I prod myself. But, studying Seale, I find there are larger issues and perhaps the answers are written elsewhere for me to learn. Reading *Seize the Time,* I hear how it is on the Panthers' side. Wondering if perhaps my unquestioned anti-militance has foundation in fact, I wander through years of *Facts on File,* drawing graphs and matching the evidence of the state against the version Bobby Seale gives. My inner adversary proceeding produces strangely reasonable doubts; and what I also find reasonable, entering Seale's mind empathetically, is his revolutionary view.

What does history have to say to this? I stumble upon Edmund Burke, whom I have never read before:

"There is, however, a limit at which forbearance ceases to be a virtue."

"We want a piece of the action," Adam Clayton Powell has said. "And we're going to get it. We're going to get it, we hope, nonviolently. We're going to get it one way or the other."

"Extremism in the defense of liberty is no vice. . . ."

Addressing the judges of England, Burke also says: "Reflect how you are to govern a people who think they ought to be free, and think they are not."

I have heard Malcolm X: "Sooner or later, when you take twenty million black people and make them fight all your wars and pick all your cotton and work all your jobs and still you never give them any real honest recompense for what they've done, sooner or later their patience and their confidence and their allegiance towards you is going to wear thin. And then you have a situation that you can't cope with."

Edmund Burke agrees: "Your scheme yields no revenue; it yields nothing but discontent, disorder, disobedience; and such is the state of America, that after wading up to your eyes in blood, you could only end just where you begun . . ."

With Rap Brown: violence is "as American as cherry pie."

And America, which always questions, "Why must I?" and answers, "I will not!" wades up to her eyes in blood.. . ."A people who are still, as it were, but in the gristle, and not yet hardened into the bones of manhood," when childhood weapons become real; and they will scream die, die at us, and act out all our fantasies.

"We shall have our manhood," Cleaver says. "We shall have our manhood or the earth will be leveled by our attempts."

"Right on, Papa Rage," says Kathleen to her man.

And yet, when France rebels, when revolution occurs there, Burke also says:

"If circumspection and caution are a part of wisdom when we work only upon inanimate matter, surely they become a part of duty, too, when the subject of our demolition and construction is not brick and timber, but sentient beings, by the sudden alteration of whose state, conditions and habits multitudes may be rendered miserable."

Time. It all takes time.

But when does forbearance cease to be a virtue? Is there a confusion in Burke; or is the difference only in revolutionary forms? And which form is Citizen Seale's? Clearly, I do not yet know enough to decide. The adversary proceeding continues, carrying me to what first seems unrelated evidence. One day, wandering among shelffuls of books, I discover long-lost poetry. It is an art form I have ignored. Metaphor and symbol are too complex for me to understand. I have needed exactitude all my life: or, I have wanted it; sluggish mind unwilling to roam free.

141

It has been an effort to associate.

But now, suddenly, a synapse has been bridged. T. S. Eliot—and Prufrock—enter my life, bringing a churning relativity:

> Let us go then, you and I,
> When the evening is spread out against the sky
> Like a patient etherised upon a table . . .

"When you grow a little older, when you get a little bolder."

> Let us go, through certain half-deserted streets . . .
> Streets that follow like a tedious argument
> Of insidious intent
> To lead you to an overwhelming question . . .

"When you live a little longer, when you grow a little stronger," when gristle hardens into bone. Then:

> Would it have been worth while,
> To have bitten off the matter with a smile . . .

"Go out into the streams, into the rapids . . ."

> To have squeezed the universe into a ball
> To roll it toward some overwhelming question,

". . . you might get some cuts along the way and some bruises"

> To say: "I am Lazarus, come from the dead,
> Come back to tell you all, I shall tell you all"—
> If one, settling a pillow by her head,
>   Should say: "That is not what I meant at all.
>   That is not it, at all."

"Remember your place."

When is there no more time?

"If I have found out, if I have found out, in spite of all that you have done, that I am not a nigger . . ."

"A little while longer," they say.

> There will be time, there will be time
> To prepare a face to meet the faces that you meet;
> There will be time to murder and create . . .

but: a time when, back from the dead, I wish to tell what I have learned only to find my truths crippled by minds grown old.

". . . what it takes to get the man off your back. What it takes to get freedom in America." The recognition of my negritude.

When is there no more time? I do not know. I must examine further documents of the court.

Then how should I begin . . .

Needing guidance from wiser minds, I go back to school, enrolling in a history course I had ignored during my degree-narrowed undergraduate days.

I have been seeing threads of continuity, a relevance of question, of issue and effect; a relevance of other lives to my own. The blacks have carried me into streams which emptied into uncharted seas for which no one has made a map. What is the further history of man? Perhaps there are some answers here. I am laden with learning of part of our world, present at all our wars for seventy years. But what happened before there was film for me to pull from the damp and shadowed archives of posthumous event?

I go back, in class, to the very beginning: to geologic time and to human time, six thousand years before, when cultivation of the earth first began, defining a state called civilized.

I hear of horror: an ancient king, capturing the invading army of a warring nation, inflicted a lesson of barbaric remembrance. He burned out the eyes of the entire army of fourteen thousand men, except for one to whom he left one eye. And then he freed his prisoners, leaving them to find their own way home, hand in hand, guided by the one-eyed man. What would the reaction have been had television been there to record the scene as the sightless army returned? Were Malmédy and My Lai better, or worse? Millennia pass. It takes time to evolve the human animal.

I learn of reformations, and go back to Burke again:

". . . the worst of these politics of revolution is this: they temper and harden the breast, in order to prepare it for the desperate strokes which are sometimes used in extreme occasions . . . the mind receives a gratuitous taint; and the moral sentiments suffer not a little. . . ."

James Baldwin says: "When one has emptied one's heart of all human feeling, you would do anything to anybody and justify it."

What happens when justice involves a war?

Writing a final paper, I find—at last—some kind of reason for Nazi Germany in Martin Luther's mandate to order, "Against the Murderous and Thieving Peasant Bands," who had found that the politics of reformation did not include a change in the brutal condition of their lives. The princes are "the rod of Christ," the civil arm. Disobedience to order is sacrilege. And in a sixteenth-century sermon, "The Tears of Germany," I find the result of reforming wars: "What shall I mention the murders and the bloodsheddings committed in every acre of ground in our land? . . . What need I relate the robberies, pillagings, plunderings of villages, cities, against promises and public oaths? What need I insist upon the general devastations by fire in every country as the armies have marched?"

". . . the earth will be leveled by our attempts."

Wolves roamed in the streets and fields of Germany, feeding off the population of a once rich and blossoming state.

". . . the mind receives a gratuitous taint; and the moral sentiments suffer not a little. . . ."

Crushed and forever bound by the Lutheran mandate, disobedience to law becomes unthinkable. In *The Rise and Fall of the Third Reich,* William Shirer writes: "Civilization came to a standstill in Germany. . . . [It] never recovered from this setback. Acceptance of autocracy, of blind obedience to the petty tyrants who ruled as princes, became ingrained in the German mind."

". . . multitudes may be rendered miserable." And die in the ovens of Buchenwald.

The woman said, "You must do as he says." In Teutonic Europe, authority reigns.

But here? In 1968, I had heard these words from the presidential candidate:

"If . . . we are going to have progress . . . you must remember that you have to have order. Because when you do not have order you have the chaotic effect of revolution. . . . You destroy more than you create. . . ."

In Watts, Newark and Detroit.

"I'm sure that many of you who have great causes . . . may say if the cause is great enough, break the law. . . ."

"If white folks is going to play Nazis, black folks ain't going to play Jews." What if Jews had broken the law?

"But . . . once you say that each man makes his own law, some man, some place in this country will make his own twisted law and we will all suffer as a result."

Should I . . .
Have the strength to force the moment to its crisis?

asks T. S. Eliot's Everyman.

"Right on, Papa Rage!"

And somewhere, some man, incubating, suddenly uncoils his own twisted law. For, like Charles Whitman, he has run out of time.

Evers is dead. Malcolm is dead. Martin Luther King and the Kennedys die too.

" . . . if the cause is great enough . . ."

But I am bothered by order too. What must we accept of the injustices thrust upon our lives? When do we give up when giving up multiplies itself?

"It all takes time."

When do we fight?

Robert Ardrey, philosopher of evolution, writes in *The Social Contract:*

"There is visible throughout all nature a bias in favor of order. . . . Order invests all living processes. . . . Order will be imposed upon disorder. And we shall return to more primitive political dispensations in which the citizen submits to violent impositions beyond his power to challenge, and keeps the peace because he must."

And Theodore White in *Caesar at the Rubicon:* "If men cannot agree on how to rule themselves, someone else must rule them."

There are separate, contending parts of me: "safety and

145

security and money" in battle with my negritude. I do not agree with myself. I am in an inner civil war. Whoever wins, I will lose. Order. Disorder. Is my American dream now in danger of perishing; unable to rule myself I must submit to violent impositions beyond my power to challenge. And keep the peace because I must.

The clock ticks:

> And the afternoon, the evening, sleeps so peacefully!
> Smoothed by long fingers,
> Asleep . . . tired . . . or it malingers . . .
> But though I have wept and fasted, wept and prayed,
> Though I have seen my head (grown slightly bald)
>   brought in upon a platter,
> I am no prophet . . .

Do I—not matter?

> I have seen the moment of my greatness flicker,
> And I have seen the eternal Footman hold my coat,
>   and snicker,
> And in short, I was afraid.

Like J. Alfred Prufrock, I have been measuring "out my life with coffee spoons." The liquid has a bitter taste.

> And I have known the eyes already, known them all—
> The eyes that fix you in a formulated phrase . . .

"I'm artist. Man. American. . . ."

> Do I dare
> Disturb the universe?

Is there progress when one dares: progress forward or falling back? What will I loose upon myself if, in a challenge to the universe, I must break the death grip on my coat; if, in order to be free, to have my negritude, I must swing myself in a bloody arc, amputating the fingers which are holding onto me?

> And when I am formulated, sprawling on a pin,
> When I am pinned and wriggling on the wall

146

Then how should I begin . . .

Prufrock evolves a gospel peculiar to his own trembling theology. Is my country—am I—"still but in the gristle," bones not yet hard enough?

And indeed there will be time . . .

Edward Brooke says, "Your place on this earth is any place you want to make it." But what happens when place has been, forcefully, denied?

I return again to Bobby Seale. In *Seize the Time,* he tells a Newton tale, an answer to the question: " 'Why do you want to be a vicious animal like a Panther?' Huey would break in. 'The nature of a panther is that he never attacks. But if anyone attacks him or backs him into a corner, the panther comes up to wipe that aggressor or that attacker out.' "

Can little white girls be Panthers too?

Seale sings a song: "Uncle Sammy Call Me Fulla Lucifer":

"You school my naïve heart to sing red-white-and-blue-stars-and-stripes songs and to pledge eternal allegiance to all things blue, true, blue-eyed blond, blond-haired, white chalk white skin with U.S.A. tattooed all over."

Not only you, Bobby Seale. They have tattooed me too. We both have numbers on our arms. But I am still in the process of evolution, "a naturistic change," and thus have not learned yet exactly where, in our nation's decimal system, I belong.

And how should I begin?

Quietly one day.

Lazarus rises from the dead: Eldridge Cleaver, who returns with *Soul on Ice* to shatter the peace of my sleeping afternoon with a sudden explosion beneath the earth: levels of being rumble and clash, trying to adjust themselves. They are to fail. The break is finality.

"Yet I may believe that a man whose soul or emotional apparatus had lain dormant in a deadening limbo of desuetude is capable of responding from some great sunken well of his being, as though a potent catalyst had been tossed into a critical mass.

... What a deep, slow, torturous, reluctant, frightened stirring!
... He feels himself coming slowly back to life. His body chemistry changes and he is flushed with new strength."

But Cleaver is also warning me: "Getting to know someone, entering that new world, is an ultimate, irretrievable leap into the unknown. The prospect is terrifying. The stakes are high. The emotions are overwhelming. The two people are reluctant really to strip themselves naked in front of each other, because in doing so they make themselves vulnerable and give enormous power over themselves. . . . How often they inflict pain and torment upon each other! Better to maintain shallow, superficial affairs; that way the scars are not deep. No blood is hacked from the soul."

> We have lingered in the chambers of the sea
> By sea-girls wreathed with seaweed red and brown
> Till human voices wake us, and we drown.

The Austrian, long in a limbo of desuetude, is Cleaver's cloistered counterpoint: "I cannot breathe," he says. "I run away from it." No stream will sweep him, out of control, to the dangerous machine of me.

But I am traveling fast, swimming with the current, following where the current leads; trusting to my own natural buoyancy; learning to trust the power of my own strengths as I move swiftly into destined time.

And now, captured by the joy of motion, I notice that I have not noticed summer pass. Suddenly, it seems, the air freshens and cools. Fall has begun.

My friend Leah, troubled by strange symptoms of caring the Austrian is producing in me, attempts to deflect me to a safer, more appropriate course. Still testing myself, I am open to the idea. I will, perhaps, be able to share more easily what it seems I am becoming with one of my own. After Saturday sundown, then, I meet with the orthodox Jewish lawyer, who politely apologizes for the fact that religious rule precludes an earlier time.

As strangers will, we discuss our work. I give a list of my involvements, to which he only half listens. He is engrossed in the

148

hatchet turns of the Hutchinson River Parkway, guiding the purring car through the suburban evening. I limn them all: Abernathy, Bond, Brooke, Brown, Eldridge Cleaver . . .

My date signals a turn. "Cleaver"—he clips his words—"is a stupid man."

My companion is a successful lawyer. Obviously he must be intelligent. I believe it is simply a question of semantics.

"Did you read *Soul on Ice?*" No one who read that book could think its author stupid, though I, myself, still do not agree with his haze-filmed philosophy.

"I don't have to read it," he says. Cleaver is pro-Arab, therefore "he hates the Jews." By application, then, "all those niggers are stupid."

I am stunned by his syllogisms. The tools of law are fact, reason and logic. In Anglo-Saxon development, the presumption of innocence is basic to the freedom we all must share; its overthrow is a pronouncement of suffering upon all of us.

Intellectually at first, then heated more and more by belief, I launch into the analogies between all hatreds: the hatreds of one nation for another; the hatreds between generations; the hatreds of race and the hatreds of one religious group for another: Catholics against Protestants against Jews against Buddhists against Hindus against the followers of Muhammad. We are first-generation American Jews, both terrifyingly conscious that our murder has been caused by centuries of madmen who, by an act of psychopathic will, have overthrown the mandates of reason and logic that are the moral law. We are both cherished children, education bought by sacrifice. Our backgrounds are exactly the same. Yet one of us is alien here.

In spite of facts, my analogies are invalid to him. He will not see. The evening turns into a disaster, and we wind up letting blood in an uncivil war. "Shiksa, goyim!" Willing my own death as a member of Rap Brown's "Fourth Reich." His contempt falls on me like a twentieth-century murrain. He says I am denying my Jewishness. But the world will not forget. "They're all Nazis. They'll come after us again. No matter what you say, next time you won't be safe."

149

In my turn, I accuse. "You're a lawyer. What do you do? Do you volunteer your skills to ADL? Do you fight?"

"No." Proud collector of a massive library of Judaica, he sits at home and reads our dusted histories. "And every evening, straight from work, I go to synagogue and pray."

Ah, I think, the ancient ways. With the tablets of law he stones himself. You will not get involved in your own defense. That is exactly how six million died. You have allowed the world to inject a paralytic agent into your mind, a hallucinogen of belief in your own weakness. Like any group proud of its traditions, we are "different," therefore strange, therefore to be feared, therefore to be hated. The equation goes in a straight line. Xenophobia is an enduring trait. And you believe there is nothing you can do! Coward, fearful of a strength you think greater than your own, you have let them emotionally emasculate you; and despising your own impotence, you turn your hatreds outward, victim of the same disease that has victimized you. The world is filled with niggers who are all stupid. You, certainly, are not to blame for the tragedy of being born a Jew.

Silently, I mourn the lawyer's shattered soul; the fossil in which I see the Ice Age of my people. Both of us carry, deep within, the urns of Auschwitz. But I have also been in the trenches of Philadelphia, Mississippi, and on the streets of Selma; and I now understand that without the privilege of these journeys into strange and alien worlds, this man will forever remain within that silent, anachronistic room whose ancient books he has formed into walls of electrified barbed wire.

"You have to be careful. But you can't allow yourself to become paralyzed by fear."

You must fight for yourself, or else you die. Rap Brown's methods are not mine, but I would not dumbly march to their barked command, should the Reich come here. It is you, in the end, I think, they will lead, shuffling silently without a word, again into the ditches above which machine guns sound.

Our respective angers are too intense to last. Burning out, we quiet down and arrive, finally, where we set out to go. Shaken by the discovery that there is no place for me anywhere, even among my own, I order a martini, double strength. The lawyer says nothing, but in his expression I see confirmation of his belief. Thesis proved. Only *schvartzes* and the *goyim* drink like that.

"The total white America can not tell the truth about herself."

On journeys into strange new worlds, one by one companions die. The hazards of risk—what exploration is—involve fatal calamity.

"If she did, she would have to commit . . . suicide. . . . That might not be such a bad idea."

But saviors are suicides too. Are they given entrance to heaven when they die? Or are they also denied that brave new world?

"People are free as they wish to become."

> Do I dare
> Disturb the universe?

"The problem is the price."

> In a minute there is time
> For decisions and revisions which a minute will reverse.

I have not much time to decide on time. I am an endowed citizen, the electorate of Oz. And soon, soon, I must cast my vote . . . or give it up, living an exile forever in my own never-never land.

"No country can survive. No country can survive!" James Baldwin says. James Baldwin has been right before.

⨎ 3

Suddenly, I am helpless against my will. I am in battle all the time,

> . . . time to murder and create . . .

"Life was never intended to be a stagnant pool," the senator has said. Has he meant this? I am in danger constantly of tidal waves I cannot stop. An insidious question gathers force: am I the victim of what is rolling over me, or am I the wave itself: destroyer or destroyed?

Bursting with successive rage, I fight everyone, even those whose knowledge, I know, is greater than mine.

One evening, my instructor informs us that he wishes to short a class so that we may all attend a Vietnam demonstration day; and, in class, rushes through a century I have come to learn about in order to lecture on the evil of American ways. My apoplexy matches his own. Unable to be silent, I shoot up my hand, demanding why I must pay tuition to listen to the mea culpas he makes to us. I feel no guilt. I will most certainly not pay for his.

"Surely you don't believe in war?" His answer is incredulous.

"Being *for* war is like being *against* motherhood," I answer back: his reasoning is incredible. I am filled with anger at the lack of insight into the very learning he is giving us. Words burst from me relentlessly as I proclaim the principle of self-interest from which no nation can, nor should, nor must be immune. I no longer believe in the messianic virtue we make of our own childhood fantasies of omnipotence. We are a living nation, ungodlike, like all the other nations and peoples of the world. I see no need to rip my flag to shreds because I have discovered its stripes and stars are composed of materials that are less than colorfast. I am far beyond my own masochistic states. I am human. So what? So are we all. It is a relief to be able to make mistakes, for that is what chance and risk involve. "Pain is part of growing up." True human evolution inevitably brings with it some kind of agony.

The rest of the class is silent. But I renounce this forced subjugation to the liberal will. I demand my lesson in history: the facts. I will decide for myself. His proselytizing here is anarchy. I want my lesson. Or I will have something to say about this class!

The instructor, stunned, is unprepared for this disagreement on principle. He is silent for a moment: a pasty man: flabby, soft. He smiles weakly, and then apologizes to us all. He understands the foundation for my objection, though he cannot see the structure which stands on it.

"She is right," he says. "You have paid for the class." And turns back to the books of time, to tell us how it has been, not how he would make it be if he were the elect of the world.

". . . try to walk as far as you can by yourself," the senator has said; even if you must always walk alone. But the cost is truly terrible. I cannot stand what I feel. The days grow short. They get colder all the time. But I am caught in an oven I do not understand, the furnace of myself like a cauterizing mechanism, searing my own history. I feel pain all the time. Where will I get "the strength to force the moment to its crisis," before I grow too old to dare, and my little pool of courage dries as do the juices of my glands?

Cleaver has tongs around my soul. I cannot shake him free. He is Bessemered-steel and will not melt, no matter how far I drag him into flame. It is Cleaver who is dragging me. And one day brings me to *The Seven Storey Mountain* for a meeting with Thomas Merton, the monk who, above the treeline, points a retributive finger and forces me to face the howling storm: the iced mirage blazed upon my retinas: the other ghettos "where all the senses and imagination and sensibilities and emotions and sorrows and desires and hopes and ideas of a race with vivid feelings and deep emotional reactions are . . . bound inward by an iron ring of frustration."

On my own mountain in Vermont the iron ring had begun to break. It was only a year before.

"In this huge cauldron, inestimable natural gifts, wisdom, love, music, science, poetry, are stamped down and left to boil with the dregs of an elementally corrupted nature."

The cauldron bubbles, nearing term.

"Revolution is nothing more but evolution," Gregory says.

The Force of Time.

"Evolution is a gradual naturistic change. It leads into revolution, which is quick change."

A war with the universe: the inevitability of death perhaps.

"Nature's law is when you are nine months pregnant she is going to drop this baby if it means death to the mother and the child."

Adam Powell says "Now. Now. Now!"

An omnipotent order circles me, eyes like bits of blue glass threatening: "Shiksa, goyim, *achtung* Jew." The female procreates herself, while guttural voices shout, "Die, Nigger, Die!"

"If I have found out, if I have found out . . ."

Hush, child, don't answer white folks back. Stay in line. You'll anger them.

I want to play. I want to eat . . . I want recognition of my negritude! I am woman, contemporary, American. Inestimable natural gifts stamped down; nature elementally corrupted by the rules: You must do as they say.

Why must I? Why?

And now a potent catalyst is tossed into the near-critical mass.

The bubbling cauldron is about to explode. A rage to live threatens my life.

The inner storms are too much for me. Frightened, I run to the Austrian again. He is my cove, my shelter.

"I say the only thing to put out fire is
    water!"

The Austrian will know what I should do. Long-boiling pressures are beginning to erupt. The linking relativities give me no peace. I can no longer stay within the confines of my job. There is a great deal I wish to say. There is a great deal I must say.

I am Lazarus, come from the dead,
Come back to tell you all,

I must tell you all! I am still afraid. Reason and logic tell me I will be terribly alone in this new world, isolated from humanity not only in the process of saying what I must, but also by the words I speak. They will call me *shiksa, goyim* again. "What makes you such an authority?" Those I know and cherish tell me I must be mad. I have everything. I never punch a clock. I am free. Expectations, rising, certainly will be met. I will have even more in following years. "That's a lot of money for a girl."

I am not—a girl! I am grown: an adult, a woman seeking possession of herself. "Why throw it all away?" I must. I must. I can't give up.

The Austrian will understand. Has he not, after all, understood before? With whom else have I ever been able to strip naked the terrible imaginings of my mind? To whom else have I ever been able to expose my hidden self?

"Will it help you to speak to me?" he says.

"Yes." It always has. But I do not speak these three last words, for thoughts such as these must remain unspoken. He has forbidden me to feel this way: " . . . I cannot breathe."

I will not force him before his time. Just months before, restless and rebelling against the rigid schedule he had imposed, I had called one Sunday to protest.

155

"I want to talk to you." I had no time for subtlety. The words, unbidden, came rushing out.

"I am tired. I wish to go back to bed. You should watch the tennis matches on television."

"I don't want to watch the tennis matches. I want to talk to you."

"But I don't want to talk. I want to go back to sleep. Some other time."

Angered, I had begun to list the catechism of his sins. But he had refused to be drawn into argument.

I had outlined one.

"Right," he answered.

And still another.

"Right," he answered again.

And another: his refusal of concession on every point growing in importance as I spoke.

"Right."

"I am trying to understand you."

"Right. I am well and alive."

He had promised, and then refused.

"Well, so it does not work like this. I am superficial and selfish, I tell you that. We shall have to think of something else. But another time. Now I go back to bed."

I want a recognition of my rights in this relationship. And I want it now. Now. Now!

"Well. So you cannot have it now." His voice, never rising, still carried something that frightened me. "I do not wish to talk now. You must watch the tennis matches on television. I go back to bed."

Why must I? But it had been no use. Like one ominous, repeated note, a drumbeat, his answers had traveled, echoing, through the Sunday afternoon. It is not yet time. I had been very angry. But there had been something there I had not understood, had never felt in him before. And, in short, I was afraid. "Right." Wrong! Something wrong. Slamming down the telephone, I had curled up on the couch, under the laden bookshelves, and I, too, had gone to sleep.

156

"Will it help you to speak to me?" now he says.

"Yes." It always has. I do not speak these three last words. I have been warned. But I also understand.

> . . . I have heard the mermaids singing, each to each.
> I do not think that they will sing to me. . . .

They sing, they sing. There is a melody, a lyric testament of compassion: a metronome that ticks, readjusting itself.

"Black folks in America have got a callus round their soul."

He does not hear: but the ticking of his clock, his jagged time, becomes a throbbing rhythm in my life. I have often seen him silent, leave a room, to walk upon the beach while the grunions spear and stab at him. I will say nothing. I will not say that I have seen him "formulated, sprawling on a pin."

"Pain is part of growing up." Grief is born in solitude. "The SS took him away."

Over the telephone, there is the soft, almost whispered voice to which I have grown so accustomed this past year. "Will it help you to speak to me?" He speaks in accents of some world which I have yet to find, yet whose language is, in me, somewhere genetically familiar and subconsciously understood.

But as I drive over the Queensboro Bridge to his home, past the tall riverside apartment buildings, past the bread-making factories from which there will soon, in just a few hours, float the odor which teases my memory with sunshine afternoon walks home carrying a brown paper bag, dipping into it to claw beneath the crackling crust, unable to resist evisceration of the loaf: as I drive, brake and double-clutch around the twisted spiral turns leading off the bridge, I wonder if I am not making some terrible mistake. There is a sense of apprehension. I am not calm. I am not at peace. I cannot even handle my car well: the gears grind: I shift too high, too low. I cannot get the sound of engine revolutions right.

Still I continue, driving into the far reaches of Queens where he lives in a modern apartment house with a tinkling lobby fountain whose waters recycle themselves in a concrete and plastic shell. It is very quiet here. Unlike my cacophonous neighborhood, there is no one on the streets at night. There are, however, trees and lawns. Even the air smells different.

Smiling, gaily he welcomes me at the door. We begin to talk. Together we explore alternatives, outline arguments for and against. Patient, thoughtful, he listens far into the night.

Suggesting, counseling at first, he then grows silent as my discordant feeling builds, begins feeding off itself.

I talk of an undeniable core, the churning, bubbling heat of some illogical destiny; and of the inner voices which say, counter to all the clarified images before our eyes: which say we must; which say to dare. But do I? Do I dare? I do not have his gifts, the charismatic quality I have noticed in the lodge where each half-smiled suggestion of his is adopted; where he can push off down a mountain, without a word or a command, to find himself followed by a long line of the rest of us. Somehow, he has always co-opted the point; somehow we have always given it to him.

I question his own ambitions. He has worked for the same company for eleven years; the company he had joined just out of school in Europe. "Don't you want something else?"

"I better not, " he says. "It is the only thing I know how to do."

"But perhaps you can do something more, try something else. Are you always going to stay in the same place? You can do anything you want."

He shrugs his shoulders. "I do not want to be President of the United States."

No. He could not be that. But to be at the very top of something: to stand on the furthest peak of the world.

"It is too much trouble up there," he says. Leaning back on the foam rubber couch, he sips straight Scotch from a tall glass and flicks ashes from an endless succession of cigarettes into an overflowing ceramic dish. He has methodically prepared himself. On one side of the slatted wood table is a stack of Camels, neatly arranged. Camels? I thought no one smoked them anymore. Unfiltered cigarettes are too dangerous.

Unable to sit still, I begin to pace up and down the barren studio apartment in which he lives. The feeling, derived from other sources I have not yet recognized, makes me very restless.

Poking, prying, contending, I present arguments of myself to him.

"We have to go as far as we are able to."

"Why?"

"Because we must. Because each of us has something. God gave it to us. We must use it."

"Well. So you will earn points in heaven."

"But you must try too."

He leans forward idly, more engrossed with punching buttons on a small cassette machine than with answering me. He inserts a cartridge, changes his mind, pulls it out and selects another one. The music, a diluted rock, sounds to me more like an ill-matched amateur orchestra, tuning up, trying to find a key in which there is an approximation of mutual knowledge.

We cannot deny these things in ourselves. There are all sorts of ways to create. I want to be the architect: the designer of the plane. I must get back what's lost to me. They have, somehow, stolen it away. They do not hear.

Trembling at my own reactions, and his denial of them, I stand over him, bent with pain. He shakes his head, studying me.

"Crazy. You are a crazy woman." Reflecting . . . then he says, "Well, you wish to write. That cannot be explained. What must one expect of you but to be crazy?"

Crazy?

Put away. Asylumed.

Alone.

I begin to cry. I am . . . a human being. I feel. A little word. Everything I have been commanded not to say now comes pouring out in a great deluge of Gregorian black: words heard a year ago suddenly booming from a track etched forever in my mind. ". . . a free man is a man with no fears . . ."

He is contemptuous of these black truths. They are only words on film. Do you really believe what you see on movie screens?

"And what do you believe in?"

"I believe in myself. I have no fears. I take care very well. It is only that I have time only for very little adventures. I am busy. I run here and there," he outlines. "Soccer, tennis, skiing, work

. . . Always there is something which I must do. I come here only to sleep. Sometimes—once or twice a month—I will take an evening off. But then I wish only to be alone."

In the L-shaped room, there are no pictures anywhere. The modern teakwood bar—set against a wall truncated by entrances to bath and sleeping alcove—is filled entirely with quarts of Scotch. They are all Johnny Walker Red. No one else, I think, drinks here.

I feel another sort of self-created camp. It is growing very late and I am exhausted by the recurrent image. One cannot liberate those to whom slavery is more necessary than freedom. But when I turn to leave, he leads me to a table piled high with dusty, leather-covered books. They are first editions which someone has just given him. Slowly he turns the pages for me. The lithographs are very beautiful; carefully he lifts the dried, crackling tissue paper off each one. The books are all in German.

"I just get them yesterday. An old Swiss man gave them to me. I go all the way upstate to bring them back. It is a long drive. But they are . . ."

He smiles, running flexible fingers over the pages and the rich brown bindings of the books. I have shown him the few first editions I have, the Stanley diaries of exploration my father cherished and left to me.

"They are like yours," he says, almost shy.

I smile back at him; and then, both temporizing at the door, we begin to indulge ourselves in the private game we had acknowledged long before.

> Let us go then, you and I,
> When the evening is spread out against the sky
> Like a patient etherised upon a table.

In the precision skills of *Kriegspiel,* the Austrian and I are perfectly arrayed. In the background, the orchestra has come together now and liquid voices begin to sing.

> There will be time, there will be time . . .

But dawn nears: the end—or the beginning—of the day; and in

this disputed hour the light becomes insidious.

> Oh, do not ask "What is it?"
> Let us go and make our visit.

From the shadows, Time beckons us against our wills; and the maneuvers we make together around the room turn themselves into a dance macabre. Circling each other back and forth across the floor, the tenuous actions of mutual need are no longer muted by protective shields. What is there turns childhood's games to war, and blood streaks the room from scars that each of us hacks deep.

We draw each other to defeat. In a moment of détente he softly asks, "How must I be for you?" I answer him, but I have mistaken the meaning of the lull. For with my answer the earth shakes again with a final, deafening ambuscade.

"I cannot! I would have to give everything up."

"What would you give up?"

"My whole . . ." He cannot say the word. "I would have to give up . . ." he turns away, ". . . my life!"

> . . . No! I am not Prince Hamlet, nor was meant to be. . . .

The mermaids will not sing to me, rocking me to sleep, he says. The mermaids have been taken away: the SS tracked them down and with seaweed choked off their life. I can still hear them scream: mermaid bodies do not decay. They lie there forever on the beach, forever wreathed with seaweed which is maggoted by time into the contagious air: "I cannot breathe . . ."

The legacy of helplessness. Stay in line. "Safety and security . . . No country can survive. No country can survive!"

Ah, Austrian, you will shatter on the high notes of the universe. You are not alone. There are others strung beside you, held by the same brittle garrote wire.

"The very notion of change, real change, throws all Americans into a panic . . ."

"Entering that new world is an ultimate, irretrievable leap into the unknown." And out in that unexplored atmosphere, following invisible tracks of self, there are no maps, no charted roads.

161

We might fall off the edge of the world. No one will hear our screams. Alone, driven out, isolated from our own kind, no one will come and save the defenestrated little lost child.

And the afternoon, the evening, sleeps so peacefully!
Smoothed by long fingers,
Asleep . . . tired . . . or it malingers . . .

and order invests the processes of the land. "The problem is the price."

"I would have to give up my life!" And giving up multiplies itself.

"I cannot!" he says. It is my screams that now he hears. The Austrian, too, has his Kristallnacht. He is too fragile. I must go. I have no more time. The notes link themselves together at last: the music of my negritude. I hear it now, now, now! And I must plunge myself into the cacophonous symphony, climbing the notes onto the peaks where the air is fresh, new, glittering. I must become my dream.

And so, stepping carefully among the jagged shards, I leave a bloodied spoor upon the wasteland that has been our battleground; and, gliding past the lobby fountain whose waters softly, endlessly splash in the concrete shell, I point my car onto the deserted highways whose interconnections will bring me swiftly home.

Another journey still. And not the last. Somehow I am always going away.

"You are so tame now," once he said, not recognizing that I had felt his strength and his strength had calmed my fear. And now, Lazarus, returned from the dead, I have seen him ". . . formulated, sprawling on a pin . . . pinned and wriggling on the wall . . ." He will not allow me to tell him all: to tell him of the pictures that I see. I have been there too; helpless, isolated and alone.

I have had a callus round my soul. There is no more time. I have burst free. The naturistic change finishes with its self. I am the casualty, the bloodied survivor of my own revolutionary war.

"The problem is the price. The price a white man and a white woman . . . will have to pay in themselves before they can look at me as though I were just another human being . . . This metamorphosis is what we are really striving for . . ."

It takes a human being to see. The shattered Austrian has pointed mirrors of himself at me. The glass is clouded, smoked by flame and tragedy; and on its surface now wavers, floats indistinct, only the shadow of a man. I cannot remain looking, like Narcissus, drowned by my Austrian self.

I have become: woman, contemporary, American. I will look for, explore, artistry. The cocoon has burst, ripped open by the jagged, blackened glass. And all the soldiers on the face of the earth cannot stop the revolution of my will.

"People are free as they wish to become."

When is there no more time?

When "I have found out that I am not a nigger, and that you invented me because you needed me . . ."

Perhaps Rap Brown is right: "I say violence is necessary . . ."

I must back the system up. I cannot deny myself. No longer silent, I must speak. And if my angered words, my truths, bring me too close to the points of steel, I will find ways to save myself. "Never again!" An American is a survival form.

"Why go to the moon?" the President asked. Because, in the legends of America, the moon is the ladder to the furthest star. It is out there waiting. And if the sounds of love shatter the peace of night, it is but the crashing of the barrier to the sky.

Crossing, finally, the threshold of my home, I find that though I am very tired, I cannot get to sleep. There is not much time. I must rest a little first. But as I toss out there in space, Prufrock and I meet for the last time in a final dialogue. On the running magnetic track, black voices sing: the music of *Romeo and Juliet.*

It is with the Austrian that I have my curtain fantasy. He stands in a shaded pool of light, his dancer's form hovering: a shade of pain. Slowly, in the evanescent dark, I perform a lingering epiphany.

"Let us go then, you and I," I say, dreaming to him of some mountain washed by a rainbow sky where our child is born: the little boy with Mongol eyes who looks like him.

"Let us go then, you and I," I say, leaving behind the ancient streets; streets that, with mad intent, turn back twisting into time

163

to lead us once again to fired underbrush where, separately, we will die.

He will not listen to what I say. He turns the downward mouth away. And the journey continues, to the end. I turn:

"Oh, I would write and plant and mend, and bring you great comforters at the bend of each long brilliant day; and you would draw your family up around your ears and soundly sleep; and I would pray, in the middle of the night, to make it day throughout your life."

He will reach for me no more. Daybreak creeps across the floor: the mountain hides and the sky lowers itself, like a compression upon my chest.

"I have dared, dared the universe for you. It has promised me you and then, tauntingly, taken you away: leaving in its place the jagged space where you once stood."

The soft brush of skin against my cheek; the clothed strength of your arms; the swift hidden look that seeks, flashes sunshine and in a minute, remembering, takes its visions and is gone.

Day breaks. The mountain dissolves. I am all alone once more on the flat and emptied plains of Oz. There is no one here but me. And the little baby boy has died.

I grow old . . . I grow old . . .

and pain sucks at my lingering strength. I have learned the price of dreams: unprotected by the Austrian, there is danger at the frontier. The conquest of Oz is the conquest of fear. All great explorations are. And if I fall off the edge of the world, it is still to the edge of the world I go: the manifest American destiny.

To get there—ah, Austrian—what I must give up is . . . you.

It is early morning. The gray beginning light of winter seeps through the windowpanes. I turn away from it to the wall. I will have to seize the time. But now I curl up in my shadowed place and, exhausted, go to sleep.

164

An Epilogue

Manhattan Island is nearly not an island at all. The great ocean to the east divides and subdivides itself repeatedly as its slivered fingers twist around the land. The Atlantic becomes New York Bay, which, in one direction, squeezes past Governors Island through Buttermilk Channel to continue narrowly into the East River. At Hell Gate there is still another division: the East River becomes the Harlem River, which looks more like a high-walled moat; and it is the Harlem River which, at the blunted northern tip of Manhattan, only barely separates the Island from the hills of the Bronx. It is the Harlem River, too, suddenly taking this sharp western curve, which links itself finally to the legendary Hudson, up which the primitive ships sailed during the series of explorations which led, eventually, into the vast interior of America.

Manhattan Island is one borough in the City of New York, port of entry for the world. The City is both inter- and intra-national. It is called "The Big Apple," "Baghdad-on-the-Subway." It is also called "Fun City," the name spoken with bitter irony by those who find it a nightmared dream.

The truth is somewhere in between. If the glistening minarets

165

of Baghdad cast a call to other continents at other times, in Baghdad beggars layered the streets, thieves hid in dark passageways . . . and the garbage never was collected at all.

If Baghdad was, then, a jewel with many flaws, so too is the City of New York: the most obtrusive of the treasures collected by a civilization which began only seconds ago, as time is measured by those who measure time. But the jewel, like a pitted bearing, lies within the central mechanism of a curious magic lantern whose often irregular images are compressed or elongated from their accepted shapes like mirrors in an amusement park. And it is from the pictures of this city that we are able to forecast the future world. In New York City, the future is always now.

If, then, the Greater City is the basic mechanism in our lens, so, too, is Manhattan Island—within the City itself—its most primal element. For here on this island, so narrowly escaped from peninsulardom, stand all the sets against which we set ourselves. Manhattan Island makes our definitions very clear.

Other cities make their separations with euphemistic geography: Beverly Hills and Watts tell us precisely who lives where—and why. The surrounding boroughs of New York City have euphemisms of their own: Bedford-Stuyvesant and Bay Ridge. And there are euphemisms on the Island too: Chelsea, Turtle Bay, Hell's Kitchen, Greenwich Village, Soho and Harlem. But at the very center of the Central City, where final power is resolved, the names become even simpler, more precisely redolent of our history: East Side, West Side: moving from constitutionally originated states of being to lands less civilized, less subject to law, richer in undiscovered possibility. Go west.

At least, it was that way until recently, when history began another cycle and the rush for gold once more began.

I live on the West Side of the Island. But it has been home to me for many years, a base from which to launch myself to further expeditioning which, somehow, seemed to promise more. But I have been to the rainbow now and I have found that what is there is only a cauldron of fools' gold.

I do not wander anymore. For the past two years my journeys have all been here: and daily I have watched, within the narrowed prisms of my sight, as the population began to change; as the old landmarks, built in a more gracious age with the accumulated knowledge of centuries, have been torn down one by one, replaced by ponderous slabs of concrete and glass; as the voices on the street lost the gift of tongues and became suddenly intelligible; as the decibeled street music ended, flattened to a single note in a universal key.

I hear America singing, the varied carols I hear.

Walt Whitman wrote in, and of, our unbirthed conceptual age.

That music always round me, unceasing, unbeginning—
yet long untaught I did not hear. . . .

The varied carols now are gone. It is easier for me to sing this song. It sits more comfortably on my own vocal chords. But I wonder what will happen when the mirroring Island clouds in desuetude; when soothed, sleeping, it malingers in the dusted air through which threads the *Nachtmusik* of Manhattan. Now become a lullaby.

When you live a little longer,
when you grow a little stronger . . .

I am no longer ceaselessly mobile. I am immersed in the voyages of other human beings: the travels of the mute. And if I am silent once again, it is only because now I am listening.

"I hear America singing . . .

"I do not think the performers know themselves—but now I think I begin to know them."

And now I find I must strain for sounds of the human voice; to hear the American song.

I do not go to films much anymore; I seldom work in film libraries. There are times, however, when elements I cannot control make me seek answers again from the color screen. Times like a heavy, laden day last spring, on the twelfth of June, 1972, when the still, unmoving air enveloping the City weighed too heavily upon my chest. It had become difficult to breathe. Soaked

167

by an ephemeral, ominous sense memory, I walked slowly, as if at half speed, to an evening picture show.

Though it was Monday, the first workday of the week, the neighborhood movie theater was strangely full. In the large, old-fashioned building with its rococo statuary, we watched an ancient vision reappear before our eyes: a modern apocalypse: a painting by the Paraclete, who is, of course, a crazy man.

The Hospital emergency room is cross-cut with violence: a snake pit of junkies who have O.D.'d; of women aborted criminally; of blacks with slashed chests from which the red blood flows; of agonized paranoids cataloging, one by one, the afflictions they see on their own wavering minds. The sudden shock of their own frailty terrorizes human beings whose bodies are wrenched from their own control. Unaware that they could die, they spiral off into uncharted space, where we cannot rescue them.

The screen darkens with tragic understanding, moving us on into contemplations of helplessness. The doctor sits in a pool of shaded, crepuscular light. It is a time when all the living are asleep. No voices interrupt the dialogue we see wrenching at the muscles of his face. He has a hypodermic and a small, deadly vial. Peace is a tiny pinprick away: a drop of blood . . . eternity. The doctor is doomed, the survivor's will destroyed. There is only the uselessness of further pain. Impotent organisms have their limits too. And the terminally ill seek death: courting, coaxing, demanding that death must hear. Death must comply! Those who have lost their voice in suffering fall in love with silence at the muted end of time.

Outside the theater, in the living rooms of the East, the last of the entertainment shows is ending. The Eleventh Hour News is about to eyewitness the world, summarizing the day as it has traveled across the curvature of the earth.

In linked capitals, secret government proceeds: on legal-sized yellow pads, presharpened pencils make the foreshadowing notes which will become our history.

In Asia, planes make craters in the earth; and then the planes fall into them.

168

In River City, the dead are dug from tombs of mud: a rising toll flashes on the screen: the body count of the electorate.

In the theater we do not see all of this as it occurs. We live, at this moment, within another world. But if, at this moment, we are not present at these other events, we soon will be. For neither are we actually living what we are witnessing now.

It is only a movie screen we watch: the flattened dimension on which an American vision presents itself. And so, as we sit in the darkened theater, we watch the protest and revolution which begins to happen before our eyes. It is filmed in the past, of the past; but it is now present as well. The illusioned nitrates of illogic explode on right and left. There is no cinematic license in what we see. The mixture of sound assaults our ears.

"We want . . ."

"You can't have . . ."

"We demand . . ."

"I refuse . . ."

Contention seethes across the screen: cross-cuts of argument flash lightning bolts as we watch a familiar story unfold.

"We will take . . ."

"I will defend . . ."

"There's no more time . . ."

"You must wait . . ."

Waves of color advance on the audience as the lasers of violence swing around. Simmering, the screen crisis erupts. And crosses invisible boundaries. Blood spurts from the film, drenching the passive spectators.

Bodies burst radially through the seats, like shrapnel from exploding minds. A battle . . . is happening.

"Where are we?"

"Are we here—or there?"

Heads turn. They swivel back and forth, from the floor of the theater to the screen. In the central audience a young black beats a seated man. The victim thrusts up his arms, helpless against the newspaper club. Sounds roar from victim and attacker, indistinguishable from noises on the screen. I cannot separate the contentions of which this sudden war is made.

169

Rooted, immobilized, I watch. There are two revolutions here. Is he a number in a file, or a face in a casting book? Is that a sound effect, or is it a real skull's cracking noise?

The missiles of rage hit, explode, opening craters as we watch. The battle makes extras of us all. We are in the script of this event. Images invade the theater. They jump at us from celluloid. A strange conception has occurred: out of reality by pretend. It has been a monstrous birth.

Somehow the disturbance ends, but we do not see the curtain scene. The healthy organism turns away from those organically deformed. The giant screen insists again and, averting our eyes, we are again automatically absorbed. The doctor's will has been reborn. He has decided to remain in life, fighting with Hippocratic rite.

Finally the movie ends, the lights go on: a dim, wire-enclosed bulb, like the exposed stamen of a flower stalk, is carried onto the stage, illuminating the worn plush seats and the candy-wrappered floor.

It is very late for a workday; and, wearily, the audience shuffles up the sloping aisle. They wander through the marbled lobby, push past the heavy, ornate doors, and slip away to their beds. They must be up early the next day, and now it is time to get some rest.

As they leave, a police car pulls out from the curb. In the wire-fenced back seat, two shackled bodies sprawl hopelessly, victimized by images cast upon a monumental screen.

"Get you up there they beat you to death."

Stunned by the relevance of visions, I too wander off. Behind me in the dark, the Paraclete lurches manically, cackling a triumphant bleat.

One day I sit fitfully before the television screen, on which are moving the transmitted views of a new city four thousand miles away. It is a city within a city, really: huge steel and cement towers into which many proud, revitalized marks have been poured.

Usually, I am fascinated by the ritual paganism of these

events, for I have long been intrigued by an equally ancient idea: the contest of champions, the death of one as surrogate for the deaths of all. A bizarre imagination had once projected the parable much further than I ever could, and flashes of *The Tenth Victim* intrude as, sporadically, I watch the Olympic Games. In the futuristic film, the ultimate sport was the hunt for man.

I am not attending closely now. The locale is too mnemonically terrible; and I cannot help casting back into history, wondering what the future will bring.

But, though our technology has brought the reels of picture more quickly now before my eyes, the hyped voices run on tracks of the past. There is no lapse of time before the future occurs again and again I watch the scene. The scene is happening now.

Munich: the ironies disinter my fear. And as I watch the mordant reenactment on my television screen, I wonder about the immutable subconscious forces that have, again, produced these deaths.

Shaken, I seek out an Israeli woman I know. Who else will be able to quiet my relapse of trembling? Who else will hear what I am beginning to hear again?

Her voice is casual, leveled, as she speaks, studying the white-ovaled fingertips interlocked comfortably before her on the table at which we sit. "Oh, we are not angry at the Germans," she says. "What else could they do, after all?"

What *else* could they do? What else could *we* do?

Nothing, in the end, an acquaintance says, practically, on another day. "There's too much oil out there," he says; and on the scales of international law, the drums of oil will always outweigh the lives of Jews.

What else can we do? Will we sign, finally, that white paper of accord, waving it once again in the wind, bringing proclamations for "peace in our time"? A small country is small price to pay.

What else can we do? Eleven Israelis have died; but of the dead, one was an Israeli by the Law of Return: the eleventh victim was an American Jew. And if he could be so easily shot down, then who among us is really safe? The living must guard the interests of life; and the dead are, after all, invisible now. The Games go on.

The lawyer was right. "They'll come after us again," he said. "Why do they always kill the Jews?" the Austrian asked. I do not know. History repeats, and in my short lifetime will I ever see a revision of its processes? If the past is to be the future once more, then what also is to be is that we will all once more be murderers: the killers will kill themselves. And the world will create and recreate its calvaries so that saviors must be born: for the need for saviors still exists. It is by lower orders that we continue to define ourselves.

"Why do they always kill the Jews?" They are assassinating us again. And, again, the Games go on.

Thoughtfully, sadly, month after month I wander from my rooms up and down, across and back the quieted City streets. I walk often late at night. There is little reason to be afraid. The high bower of new lights spreads quickly from the south, casting manufactured daylight, eviscerating the shadows so that the dark and dangerous may not hide. On my block the busy citizens link together to tap the wires, bringing the lamps onto my street. They hold meetings on security. They plant trees. On my block the niggers are all gone, carted off with their few shabby bundles by relocation agencies. And when a welfare hotel is emptied, scrubbed clean and proposed as shelter for the poor, flaring battles take place; and the citizens are able to change the intent: the apartments are assigned to the poor . . . if the poor are also old. "After all, nobody ever heard of a sixty-five-year-old junkie or an eighty-year-old mugger," proclaims a leader in the fight. "I understand your fears," says a liberal elected representative.

But I never was afraid, even when the streets were black and the triangle of land across the avenue was known as "Needle Park." I never was afraid. I am not now. Not afraid of the streets, at least. But I am growing more and more uncomfortable, for the stillness that descends is somehow more threatening.

The disappearing dark sends me into books again. The silence has become like an aural déjà vu, drawing me back nearly two centuries: to James Madison, whose comment I had first read twenty years before in an elemental history course.

"I believe there are more instances of the abridgement of the freedom of the people by gradual and silent encroachments of those in power than by violent and sudden usurpations."

Creeping steadily northward from the hub of the Central City, the lights arc over us; and, one evening, I walk slowly, sluggishly down Broadway through the illuminated evening to the colorful piazza of white stone buildings whose central fountain plays a rhythmic program of alternating waters against the backdrop of a fairy-tale Chagall.

I must board a bus to cut through the park transverse, running due east deeply into unfamiliar territory. I have a destination, but I am strangely reluctant to go. And as I step off, pushing at the self-operated doors of the bus, I find myself dawdling during the short walk south.

In the vestibule of the restaurant, I give the hovering maître d' my name. He does not need to check his list. "Ah, yes," he says, and turning smartly escorts me, purposeful and confident, through the glass-enclosed sidewalk extension, past the closely set tables covered with immaculate white cloths, to the corner where, in a heated garden setting, my dinner companion waits.

He is not waiting restlessly, though I am somewhat late. Hands clasped around a glass, he is looking into it, studying the Scotch and ice as if the striated cubes were like graphic indications he could read: as if the glass itself were like one of those scene-enclosing paperweights containing memories whose single, classic word—"Rosebud"—has become a universal chord. It is a very private moment. I am hesitant to interrupt the dialogue I see flickering across his face.

But the maître d' has many duties to perform and so, quickly, he performs this particular courtesy. He says our names as if he were introducing those who have not met before.

Jumping up, his private moment instantly cuts out. Sun breaks on the Austrian's face. Pushing back his chair, he moves quickly out of his seat, brushing my cheek with his lips; and then fusses protectively as he settles me. He orders a martini made as I prefer and then, our shoulders touching, turns and smiles.

"So. It has been a long time, no?" And immediately we fall into ease as if sinking back into an old, comfortable chair whose used cushions quickly conform to the familiar, if almost forgotten, contours we had made.

The Austrian smiles: gently and with joy. The familiar expression triggers music again: a wisp of melody, like the sound of a distant train whistle floating through the twilight air.

His face is slightly changed, though its contours remain the same. It seems less angular now; softer, more poetic. It is his longer hair, I decide; for he has given over the trimmed, boyish neatness he had when we first met, and has compromised with style to the extent that the dark hair, shaggier, frames and highlights his face.

"So. What have you been doing?" he asks, warm and concentrated again; and again, he listens closely, eyes fixed on my face, as I speak of the elapsed past. I describe my recent journeys. It is a different kind of story than I once told him: the isolation is now self-imposed so that I may wring the pictures and words from myself and set them down, for there are others who wish to see and hear. As I describe where I have been and where I am now, the Mongol eyes open wide, the circumflex mouth springs loose and he shakes his head from side to side.

"Well, well," he says, his face suffused with the soft light of the atmospheric restaurant he has picked for us. "Well, well. I do not believe you can do it. That is something. Well, well . . ." and, watching his own visions, chuckling inwardly to himself as I had often seen him do, swings his head incredulously.

We stop our talk for a moment, to select from the embossed menu and the thick, plush wine card presented to us. The Austrian orders with authority, seldom glancing to the right as he runs his finger down the list of vintages. Though I have an exacting palate, I have little scholarly interest in the various appellations and thus have never been able to apply myself to the art of fine wines. I leave selection to the Austrian, confident of his expertise. Europeans are better at this anyway, I think. They have lived with their wines from childhood days.

Around us the tables are filling up. Diners enter from two directions: from the sidewalk, through the vestibule; and also from within building recesses, funneling from the central bar. The preambles of cocktail hour are over. It is time for the rituals of dining to begin.

The dining room is bustling, but discreetly quiet. Though we sit only inches away from the others there, we hear only an occasional word. The ambiance calls for subdued voice. Even the busboys walk on cat feet here, whisking the ubiquitous bowl candles quickly off the tables, lighting them, and then setting them down unobtrusively before the busboys melt away.

The decisions of dining complete, we go on to talk of many things while we await our meal. But, as it was so long ago, we lapse again into the state of the world, exchanging views of the currents which have swept across the nation in which we live. And of the result of flood.

The Austrian has been losing his temper frequently, he says. "I am very liberal when I come here in 1965. But I see what is happening I get so angry. I explode all the time more and more. I am not so liberal as I was.

"I say to myself, you are getting just like an old man."

I tease him about that, mocking affectionately, wondering if what I hear means what I think it does. What has been happening to him?

The sommelier, dressed in a formal jacket with shining lapels, flourishes the wine gracefully, presenting its label for inspection by the Austrian. He studies it for a moment, then directs the man to pour. The sommelier watches with concern as the Austrian performs the delicate ritual: swirling the pale liquid in the glass, savoring the bouquet, tasting tentatively; thoughtfully making a decision, tasting once again before he finally nods. The wine is . . . acceptable. Smiling broadly, the sommelier serves both of us, handling the bottle with a delicate fillip so that not a single drop will spill.

The Austrian is amused. But he waits until the man leaves before he confides, "What would I do, eh, if I found I did not like it?"

175

"But you knew what you were ordering."

"Oh, no, not at all. I am not an expert. But I pretend." He chuckles confidentially, elfin-eyed and mischievous. "It is like a little game, no? He is so very serious."

I am surprised, and more than a little amused myself. The menu of this lush restaurant has its share of the classic dishes of a great cuisine. Ordering, I had, in my imagination, rolled the taste of each upon my tongue; and then decided on a richly sauced fowl. But the Austrian had picked an entrée that was little more than a steak dressed in French adjectives. And when I comment on this he says, "The Europeans, they would eat steak all the time if they could get it."

And adds: "Besides, I go to Europe last spring, I find I can't eat the food so much anymore. I am not used to it or something. My stomach bothers me. They eat too much over there anyway."

The excursion into national taste leads us back again to national politics; and, resuming, we skirmish briefly among arguments of liberal solution vs. liberal intent.

"You are in trouble now," he says. "But you have been in trouble before. It is a very strong country here. You always get out of it."

The tone of affection in his voice is something I have never heard before, particularly from members of his émigré society. He cares a great deal, he says. "I love this country. It is a second home for me. Sometimes I think I stay." And, after a long melodic pause, he adds, "Well, I just renew my contract for another three years. I try it for a little while more. I see how it goes. Then I decide, not now."

"Why did you renew your contract?" I ask. He had been due to return to Europe very soon, and had been impatiently waiting out his time.

His answer is a pounding surprise. Within the company for which he has always worked, the Austrian has a brand-new job. He has just been made head of all the operations in America.

I am stunned. It is my turn to shake my head. "I thought it was too much trouble up there for you."

He looks at me oddly, remembering, perhaps, the terminal

conversation we had had so long ago.

"They offer it to me, I think, what do I need it for? Then I think, why not? I see. But it is very difficult. Work, work. I have not the time for anything else. It is a great . . . challenge. But sometimes I think when the three years are over I will go buy a little hotel on a mountain somewhere . . . a horse, perhaps . . ." He smiles, his voice drifting off into the fresh and fragrant dream.

In the glow of the candlelight, a wash of tenderness floods my response. America sings somewhere still; her melodies, like atmospheric streams, encircling the entire globe.

> "I hear not the volumes of sound merely—I am moved by the exquisite meanings. . . ."

But he will not let me prod him further on decisions and on goals—we cannot speak of future time—and firmly shifts the conversation back onto the events and victories of my own life.

Lingering, we sit in the restaurant and eat and drink and talk until it is very late and the other diners wander out, surfeited with food, drowsing with wine. We are almost alone. It is the end of an age. We have had our meeting on the first night of our last steps on the moon. But we do not even think of laying aside our concerns to watch a television screen. There is no trumpeting television in the restaurant, as once there would have been: no throb of excitement on the streets: no fluting international chorale. The first, dangerous steps were only a short while before. But if our voyages to the edge of the world still contain great risk, the human drama has evolved into the further perfection of machines. The *Niña,* the *Pinta,* the *Santa Maria* presage the *Enterprise.*

And, at the end of the evening, when there is no more past we are able to discuss, and we are weary of present time, the Austrian escorts me to his powerful automobile and, together, we prolong the peace in a long, lazy drive through the serpentine night of Central Park.

Nothing is resolved. Nothing will ever be. We must turn ourselves from endless space to our own separate journeying. Life consists of a series of going-ons. It was that way for me, once. It was that way for the Austrian too. But going-on is not the same

177

as on-going. There are some stillnesses which are the final lingering, the final giving up; while others are but the quiet processes of sitting silent, remembering, allowing ourselves to mourn what once was and must never be again.

"I love this country," the Austrian has said. "It is a second home for me." There is no SS at the door. And if I have a certain destination, a goal always before my eyes, so too—now—does the Austrian, though he keeps his head downward bent, watching himself take each uncertain step. He has, perhaps, been infected by our dream. Is it, I wonder, only a dream of Americans; or is it really something more universal, and America is the first nation we have known to incorporate the need into a code?

But if the Austrian has become flushed with possibility, the Austrian also has lived in America for eight conflicted years. He has found out the price we pay. He has begun to pay it too. Product of an older civilization, he comes from a nation for centuries under siege. "Murderous Thieving Peasants" also roamed across his land; until the specially blessed army put down their uprisings with the sword. The Austrian is wary of the proclaimed weapons of destiny.

Yet, as I look at him, sitting comfortably and easily behind the power-fed wheel of the purring, luxurious automobile, I cannot help feeling a strange sort of pride: justification of my own contested insights, perhaps; but more, I think, a sense of wonder at my own timid messages, now amplified into discernible syllables carried over continents.

"I hear America singing." But the American anthems chorus louder now in the lands across the sea.

Months later, I wait for spring to come. The cycle repeats itself. There are floods again, and dissolving back, the television set carries a retrospective of the past twelve months. River City was an accident, manmade deaths, perhaps. But River City had forecast natural disaster with an all-too-fearful accuracy. Appalled, the scholars begin studying what we had never noticed before.

In one of the small Pennsylvania cities where the waters crumbled the monuments to a lifetime of work, drug use is up 162 percent; a surge of schizophrenia cases fill the mental wards; and there is a mounting, inexplicable incidence of sudden natural deaths. Impotent against the onslaught, fearful of future terrors which cannot be controlled, the human organisms break down: seeking the peace of chemicals, of madness, of an assured place in eternity.

At the end of June, the year of the Pennsylvania flood—two weeks after the incident at *The Hospital*—television newsman Howard K. Smith had ended an early-evening show with a commentary so precise I had called for a copy of it:

> Modern man has not done well with many kinds of problems—moral ones like war, social ones like cities. But he prides himself on his science and technology. Any problem within their boundaries he knows he can handle.
>
> Well, let his pride diminish. There are two extremely commonplace technical problems he has not, with money and research to spare, been able to touch. One is the common cold. . . . The other is even more commonplace: the weather. . . .
>
> You on the Gulf and in the Plains States know all about weather. We on the placid Atlantic have been badly shaken this week to see homes engulfed in water, cars drifting down streets turned into rivers, great dams caving in at the ends under sheets of flood water. Even the White House basement has not been immune.
>
> We end a bad week with nothing gained but one small curious insight into modern man. As waters rose and people were told to flee with only essentials, what did they grab first?
>
> Picture after picture shows men neck-deep in water grappling to save one item: the television set. Man may face nakedness or hunger, nothing but polluted water to drink. But darned if he is going to miss Marcus Welby.
>
> There's a message there. I am not sure what it is.
>
> Perhaps it is that the real life drama that moves modern man is not that which destroys his home; it is something that happens to other people on the television tube. . . .

179

Or: on the movie screen.

Early this spring, in 1973, Smith adds a hopeful note: things are getting better, he says, after a journey through America.

But in the early spring of 1973, television carries further commentary. For as the waters again begin to rise, we find there are some who will not leave their homes. They guard their possessions to the last, as the trickling waters mount to flood. The householders remain, certain that destruction "is something that happens to other people on the television tube." They are unmoved by danger. It cannot happen here. The citizens guard furniture. I have heard of that before.

But the cycle is, nevertheless, irrevocable. The rains continue, broken only by still, unmoving interludes. In New York City, this winter has been very strange. There has been little snow, few frozen days. There is something disturbing in the moderated air. The weather is unseasonal. Temperatures rise. A bank weather sign flashes numbers that cannot be: the sign must be wrong: we refuse to believe. It is very warm, but there is still no hint of spring. It is like the gray days of wintertime. A strange hush envelops the City streets once again; and once again the thick, clogging air weighs upon my chest. I walk slowly, carefully, as if approaching the boundary gates of Shangri-la, where the demands of time are a revolution challenging my immortality.

But I have been only a visitor to this fantastic mountained land, now making the Long March home. I know what waits out there. Within range of my ear, I hear the land quieting again; now hazed with Sunday indolence. We have been subject to surprise attack before: threatening our implacable security, the homes we have freely built. Will we be unprepared again?

"Passion exhausts. But love fulfills and replenishes itself." Within their camps, the armies of the night have muffled their own instruments. Are the fitful, weakening beats a last tattoo, the dying call of casualties of war from which generations of silence spring? Or are they the prelude to another sort of march, winding gently, softly, over twisting paths in a unisoned, fraternal song?

"Quicksand years," Walt Whitman wrote, "that whirl me I know not whither . . ."

"Passion exhausts . . ." The country sleeps, listless and fatigued once more. And in sleep is only fitfully aware as the atmospheres of injustice once again begin to solidify in a cycle infinitely old. There are scattered voices which push against accumulating viscosity. But resting, grateful to be still at last, we turn away and lay our flaming torches down. The voices come from a long way off: protesting, raging: they cannot breathe. And claustrophobic in the iron ring, the rooted assassin begins to churn: corrupted justice adds elements.

We cannot see him yet, or hear his voice. But he is out there somewhere, nevertheless, cataloging, one by one, the afflictions he sees wavering in the seething cauldron of his mind. If he is still and unmoving at this moment, it is because he is listening for a word; and, caught within his own created time, the past and future begin to mix, roiling on endlessly. Disposing of the present, which he does not have, he sows poisoned abrasions onto lanterns of time. The fumes of experience throw distances askew; hallucinogenic mirrors distort what he sees: acid-eaten voices sputter, spark, static with crackles of a rising rage. Words extricate themselves, sound a knell, recede, come back again. Stronger, louder, with greater clarity every time, he croons a loveless chant.

We do not know who he is. We do not know where he is. We cannot hear. We are not listening. But we must recognize that he exists. And that soon, soon again he will rise up and, in one shattering gutturality, force us to hear his rage. With a doomed power he will scar the earth, perhaps for a thousand years. And in the last, lost moments of his life, the assassin will finally free himself: in messianic fulfillment of our self-prophecies.

"They'll come after us again," the lawyer said. ". . . next time you won't be safe."

"Perhaps . . . the real life drama that moves modern man is not that which destroys his home; it is something that happens . . . on the television tube."

The assassin is out there somewhere. It is his presence we feel hovering in the brooding, ominous air. He has not yet revealed himself. But soon he will: a storm is gathering again. It will burst upon us soon. But in the living rooms on the placid Atlantic Coast, at the end of this day in early spring, we watch the weather map, set out umbrellas and rainproof coats. Tomorrow there will be rain: a slight flooding of the highways perhaps. We will be prepared for it.

And at the end of the week, worn out by our concerns, we shut off our television sets, set the windows against the rain, close off the lights. And as this day slips into past, we lay down our heads and go to sleep.

Some of us. Or, perhaps, some of us all.

73 74 75 10 9 8 7 6 5 4 3 2 1